Ninja Foodi
Max Smartlid
Cookbook

UK

Ninja Foodi Smartlid Recipes for Anyone,
A Professional Guide for Beginners,
Suitable to Many Ninja Models

Bennett Hill

CONTENTS

Chapter 4 Beef, Pork & Lamb 49

Chapter 5 Fish & Seafood 68

Chapter 7 Desserts 103

INDEX 114

INTRODUCTION

Unlock 15 cooking functions under one SmartLid, including Pressure Cook, Air Fry, Slow Cook, Grill and 5 innovative Combi-Steam Mode functions, combining steam with convection cooking for juicy, speedy and crispy results. One pot does the lot!

There's no guesswork with the integrated Smart Cook System. The Digital Cooking Probe precisely monitors your food's temperature as it cooks, so you don't have to – from rare to well done, enjoy perfectly cooked meat and fish, exactly as you like it!

Create a perfect roast chicken in under 1 hour with Steam Roast. Cook family meals in under 30 minutes.

Pressure Cook up to 70% faster than traditional cooking methods*. Auto-Steam Release completes the cooking process, totally hands-free.

Air Fry guilt-free fried food using little to no oil. Prove and bake delicious homemade bread in one pot.

Perfectly sized to feed up to 6 people, you can cook and crisp a whole 3kg chicken.

Features

3 modes, 15 functions

Unlock 15 cooking functions under one SmartLid – Pressure Cook, Air Fry, Grill, Bake, Dehydrate, Prove, Sear/Sauté, Steam, Slow Cook, Yoghurt, Steam Meals, Steam Air Fry, Steam Bake, Steam Bread and Steam Roast.

Simply switch between cooking modes using the SmartLid Slider. The lid intelligently recognises which function you are using.

Combi-Steam Mode

Discover a new way to cook, combining steam with convection for juicy, speedy, crispy results! Using the sauce, water, stock, wine or other liquid added to the pot with your ingredients, steam will infuse moisture and flavour into your food as it cooks. The result? Perfectly cooked food that's tender and moist on the inside, crisp on the outside.

Create a perfect roast chicken in under 1 hour with the Steam Roast function and Smart Cook System! Easily cook a delicious 3kg roast joint with tender, crispy results.

Cook family meals in under 30 minutes with the Steam Meals function, layering mains and sides with the 2-tier rack to create complete, delicious one-pot meals. Try Moroccan lamb steaks with Tenderstem broccoli and fluffy couscous, or perfectly cooked chicken cordon bleu with smoked ham and cheese, tender green beans and buttery mashed potato.

Steam Air Fry crispy vegetables and fresh or frozen foods like salmon fillets with steam-infused air without drying them out – enjoy guilt-free fried food that's moist and juicy on the inside, crispy on the outside. It's also perfect for quickly cooking a one-pot lasagne with a bubbling cheese topping.

With the Steam Bread function you can prove and bake perfect bread with a golden crust, all in one pot. Steam Bake quick, fluffy, delicious cakes, brioche, desserts and more.

Smart Cook System

There's no guesswork with the integrated Smart Cook System. From rare to well done, enjoy perfectly cooked meat and fish exactly as you like it with the Digital Cooking Probe.

From your favourite steaks to a whole chicken, simply insert the leave-in probe into your food and choose your desired outcome. The probe precisely monitors your food's temperature as it cooks, so you don't have to.

Pressure Cook Mode

Pressure Cook up to 70% faster than traditional cooking methods*. Pressure Cooking uses super-heated steam to quickly cook tender meals – perfect for tenderising large cuts of meat, enjoy juicy beef brisket or pulled pork in a fraction of the time.

When your food has finished cooking, Auto-Steam Release automatically releases steam to complete the cooking process. Choose from Quick, Natural or Delayed for hands-free steam release.

Air Fry Mode

Air Fry crispy fried food using little or no oil – up to 75% less fat than traditional frying methods**. Create everything from golden chips, sweet potato fries and vegetable medleys to fish fingers, chicken wings and salmon fillets.

In Air Fry mode, you can also choose from a range of other convection and hob-style functions. The possibilities are endless!

Grill tasty burgers, halloumi skewers and marinated chicken breasts. Bake fluffy cakes, cookies, pies and pastries and give cheesy pasta bakes a bubbling topping. Prove doughs to enjoy perfectly risen bread and bakes at home. Sear steaks to perfection before cooking. Sauté ingredients to prepare delicious sauces and caramelise onions for maximum flavour. Steam healthy vegetables and perfectly cooked rice. Slow Cook meals for up to 12 hours to ensure your favourite risotto, casserole or tender pulled pork is ready when you get home. Dehydrate ingredients to create vegetable crisps, dried fruit snacks, homemade jerky and dried herbs. Even create your own Yoghurt, exactly as you like it.

Easy to use and clean

Includes a 7.5L non-stick ceramic coated Cooking Pot which fits up to a 3kg roast, a 4.7L non-stick ceramic coated Cook & Crisp Basket which fits 1.8kg of French fries, and a 2-tier reversible rack – perfect for layering ingredients to cook complete meals on 3 levels, or raising food for steaming, baking and grilling.

All accessories are dishwasher safe for easy cleaning.

Helpful Hints

When following a recipe, ALWAYS use the exact amount of liquid, even when scaling down proteins or vegetables.

Refer to the Recipe Guide for exact liquid measurements for beans, grains, starches and more.

●   When using Combi-Steam mode functions, always add liquid to the pot.

●   Any liquid can be used for pressure cooking. Use broths or sauces instead of water to infuse additional flavour. Always use a minimum of 250ml of liquid. Depending on your recipe, you may need up to 750ml.

●   To convert oven recipes, use the Bake function and reduce the cook temperature by 10°C

●   When switching from pressure cooking to crisping after pressure cooking, empty the pot of any remaining liquid for best crisping results.

Pressure cooking tips

If the unit is not coming to pressure, check that the silicone ring is fully installed by pressing it into place all around the metal ring rack. Make sure the ring is completely clean and undamaged.

The time to build pressure will vary based on selected pressure, temp of the pot and temp and quantity of the ingredients (up to 20 minutes or more). Frozen and/or large amounts of ingredients will increase the time to pressure significantly (45 minutes or more).

Chapter 1 Breakfast

Soft-boiled Eggs

Servings: 4

Cooking Time: 15 Min

Ingredients:

- 4 large eggs
- 1 cups water /250ml
- Salt and ground black pepper, to taste.

Directions:

1. To the pressure cooker pot, add water and place a reversible rack. Carefully place eggs on it. Seal the pressure lid, choose Pressure, set to High, and set the timer to 3 minutes. Press Start.

2. When cooking is complete, do a quick pressure release. Allow cooling completely in an ice bath. Peel the eggs and season with salt and pepper before serving.

Breakfast Souffles

Servings: 6

Cooking Time: 20 Minutes

Ingredients:

- 1 lb. thick cut bacon, chopped
- 8 oz. pork sausage links, chopped
- Nonstick cooking spray
- 5 eggs, separated
- 1/3 cup heavy cream
- ½ cup cheddar cheese, grated
- ½ tsp salt
- ¼ tsp thyme

Directions:

1. Set cooker to sauté function on med-high.

2. Add the bacon and cook until almost crisp. Transfer to a paper towel lined plate.

3. Add the sausage and cook until done. Transfer to a separate paper towel lined plate.

4. Drain off fat and set cooker to air fry setting. Preheat to 350°F.

5. Spray 6 ramekins with cooking spray.

6. In a large bowl, beat egg whites until stiff peaks form.

7. In a medium bowl, whisk the yolks, cream, cheese, and seasonings together. Stir in the meats and mix well.

8. Gently fold the yolk mixture into the egg whites. Spoon the mixture into the prepared ramekins.

9. Place the rack in the cooker and place the ramekins on top. Secure the tender-crisp lid and bake 20 minutes, or until the soufflés have puffed up. Serve immediately.

Nutrition:

- InfoCalories 565,Total Fat 50g,Total Carbs 2g,Protein 24g,Sodium 1134mg.

Almond Quinoa Porridge

Servings: 6
Cooking Time: 1 Minute
Ingredients:

- 1¼ cups water
- 1 cup almond milk
- 1½ cups uncooked quinoa, rinsed
- 1 tablespoon choc zero maple syrup
- 1 cinnamon stick
- Pinch of salt

Directions:

1. In the Ninja Foodi's insert, add all ingredients and stir to combine well.
2. Close the Ninja Foodi's lid with the pressure lid and place the pressure valve in the "Seal" position.
3. Select "Pressure" mode and set it to "High" for 1 minute.
4. Press the "Start/Stop" button to initiate cooking.
5. Now turn the pressure valve to "Vent" and do a "Quick" release.
6. Open the Ninja Foodi's lid, and with a fork, fluff the quinoa.
7. Serve warm.

Nutrition:

- InfoCalories: 186; Fat: 2.6 g; Carbohydrates: 4.8 g; Protein: 6 g

Breakfast Pies

Servings: 4
Cooking Time: 20 Minutes
Ingredients:

- 1 ½ cup mozzarella cheese, grated
- 2/3 cup almond flour, sifted
- 4 eggs, beaten
- 4 tbsp. butter
- 6 slices bacon, cooked crisp & crumbled

Directions:

1. Select air fryer function and heat cooker to 400°F.
2. In a microwave safe bowl, melt the mozzarella cheese until smooth.
3. Stir in flour until well combined.
4. Roll the dough out between 2 sheets of parchment paper. Use a sharp knife to cut dough into 4 equal rectangles.
5. Heat the butter in a skillet over medium heat. Add the eggs and scramble to desired doneness.
6. Divide eggs evenly between the four pieces of dough, placing them on one side. Top with bacon.
7. Fold dough over filling and seal the edges with a fork. Poke a few holes on the top of the pies.
8. Place the pies in the fryer basket in a single layer. Secure the tender-crisp lid and bake 20 minutes, turning over halfway through. Serve immediately.

Nutrition:

- InfoCalories 420,Total Fat 33g,Total Carbs 3g,Protein 28g,Sodium 663mg.

Sausage & Broccoli Frittata

Servings: 10
Cooking Time: 25 Minutes

Ingredients:

- 1 tbsp. olive oil
- 1 lb. country-style pork sausage
- 4 cups broccoli florets
- 1 onion, chopped
- ½ tsp salt
- ¼ tsp pepper
- 14 eggs
- ½ cup milk
- 2 cups cheddar cheese, grated

Directions:

1. Select sauté function on med-high heat.
2. Add olive oil, once it's hot, add sausage, broccoli, onions, salt, and pepper. Cook, stirring frequently, until sausage is no longer pink. Drain the fat.
3. In a large bowl, whisk together eggs, milk, and cheese. Pour over sausage mixture.
4. Set cooker to bake function on 350 °F. Secure the tender-crisp lid and set timer to 20 minutes.
5. Frittata is done when eggs are set. Let cool 5-10 minutes before serving.

Nutrition:

- InfoCalories 374,Total Fat 27g,Total Carbs 4g,Protein 28g,Sodium 432mg.

Sweet Potato, Sausage, And Rosemary Quiche

Servings:6
Cooking Time: 38 Minutes

Ingredients:

- 6 eggs
- ¼ cup sour cream
- ½ pound ground Italian sausage
- 1 tablespoon fresh rosemary, chopped
- 2 medium sweet potatoes, cut into ½-inch cubes
- 2 teaspoons kosher salt
- ½ teaspoon freshly ground black pepper
- 1 store-bought refrigerated pie crust

Directions:

1. In a medium bowl, whisk together the eggs and sour cream until well combined. Set aside.
2. Select SEAR/SAUTÉ and set to HI. Select START/STOP to begin. Let preheat for 5 minutes.
3. Add the sausage and rosemary and cook, stirring frequently, for about 5 minutes. Add the sweet potatoes, salt, and pepper and cook, stirring frequently, for about 5 minutes. Transfer this mixture to a bowl.
4. Place the pie crust in the pan, using your fingers to gently push onto the bottom and sides of the pan. Place pan with pie crust on the Reversible Rack, making sure it is in the lower position. Place rack with pan in pot. Close crisping lid.
5. Select BAKE/ROAST, set temperature to 400°F, and set time to 8 minutes. Select START/STOP to begin.
6. Stir the sausage and sweet potatoes in to the egg mixture.
7. When cooking is complete, open lid and pour the egg mixture into the browned crust. Close crisping lid.
8. Select BAKE/ROAST, set temperature to 360°F, and set time to 15 minutes. Select START/STOP to begin.
9. When cooking is complete, carefully remove pan from pot. Let cool for 10 minutes before removing from pan.

Nutrition:

- InfoCalories: 344,Total Fat: 22g,Sodium: 743mg,Carbohydrates: 22g,Protein: 14g.

Mediterranean Quiche

Servings: 6
Cooking Time: 45 Minutes
Ingredients:

- Nonstick cooking spray
- 2 cups potatoes, grated
- ¾ cup feta cheese, fat free, crumbled
- 1 tbsp. olive oil
- 1 cup grape tomatoes, halved
- 3 cups baby spinach
- 2 eggs
- 2 egg whites
- ¼ cup skim milk
- ½ tsp salt
- ¼ tsp pepper

Directions:

1. Select bake function and heat to 375°F. Spray an 8-inch round pan with cooking spray.
2. Press the potatoes on the bottom and up sides of the prepared pan. Place in the cooker. Secure the tender-crisp lid and bake 10 minutes.
3. Remove pan from the cooker and sprinkle half the feta cheese over the bottom of the crust.
4. Set cooker to sauté function on medium heat. Add the oil and heat until hot.
5. Add the tomatoes and spinach and cook until spinach has wilted, about 2-3 minutes. Place over the feta cheese.
6. In a medium bowl, whisk together eggs, milk, salt, and pepper. Pour over spinach mixture and top with remaining feta cheese.
7. Place the pan back in the cooking pot and secure the tender-crisp lid. Set temperature to 375°F and bake 30 minutes or until eggs are completely set and starting to brown. Let cool 10 minutes before serving.

Nutrition:

- InfoCalories 145,Total Fat 8g,Total Carbs 12g,Protein 7g,Sodium 346mg.

Apple Walnut Quinoa

Servings: 2
Cooking Time: 15 Minutes
Ingredients:

- ½ cup quinoa, rinsed
- 1 apple, cored & chopped
- 2 cups water
- ½ cup apple juice, unsweetened
- 2 tsp maple syrup
- 1 tsp cinnamon
- ¼ cup walnuts, chopped & lightly toasted

Directions:

1. Set the cooker to sauté on med-low heat. Add the quinoa and apples and cook, stirring frequently, 5 minutes.
2. Add water and apple juice and stir to mix. Secure the lid and set to pressure cooking on high. Set timer for 10 minutes.
3. When timer goes off use quick release to remove the lid. Quinoa should be tender and the liquid should be absorbed, if not cook another 5 minutes.
4. When quinoa is done, stir in syrup and cinnamon. Sprinkle nuts over top and serve.

Nutrition:

- InfoCalories 348,Total Fat 12g,Total Carbs 54g,Protein 9g,Sodium 7mg.

Cranberry Lemon Quinoa

Servings: 6
Cooking Time: 20 Minutes

Ingredients:

- 16 oz. quinoa
- 4 ½ cups water
- ½ cup brown sugar, packed
- 1 tsp lemon extract
- ½ tsp salt
- ½ cup cranberries, dried

Directions:

1. Add all ingredients, except the cranberries, to the cooker and stir to mix.
2. Secure the lid and select pressure cooking on high. Set timer for 20 minutes.
3. When timer goes off, use natural release for 10 minutes. Then use quick release and remove the lid.
4. Stir in cranberries and serve.

Nutrition:

- InfoCalories 284,Total Fat 4g,Total Carbs 56g,Protein 8g,Sodium 152mg.

Cinnamon Sugar French Toast Bites

Servings: 4
Cooking Time: 10 Minutes

Ingredients:

- Butter flavored cooking spray
- 1/3 cup Stevia
- 1 tsp cinnamon
- 4 slices sourdough bread, sliced thick, remove crust
- 2 eggs
- 2 tbsp. milk
- 1 tsp vanilla

Directions:

1. Set to air fryer function on 350°F. Spray the fryer basket with cooking spray.
2. In a small bowl, combine Stevia and cinnamon.
3. In a medium bowl, whisk together eggs, milk, and vanilla until smooth.
4. Slice bread into bite-size cubes, about 8 pieces per slice. Dip in egg mixture to coat. Place in a single layer in the fryer basket and spray lightly with cooking spray.
5. Secure the tender-crisp lid and cook 3-5 minutes until golden brown, turning over halfway through cooking time.
6. Roll French toast bites in cinnamon mixture and serve. Repeat with remaining bread and egg mixture.

Nutrition:

- InfoCalories 219,Total Fat 4g,Total Carbs 34g,Protein 10g,Sodium 424mg.

Pepperoni Omelets

Servings: 4
Cooking Time: 5 Minutes
Ingredients:

- 4 tablespoons heavy cream
- 15 pepperoni slices
- 2 tablespoons butter
- Black pepper and salt to taste
- 6 whole eggs

Directions:

1. Take a suitable and whisk in eggs, cream, pepperoni slices, salt, and pepper.
2. Set your Ninja Foodi to "Sauté" mode and add butter and egg mix.
3. Sauté for 3 minutes, flip.
4. Lock and secure the Ninja Foodi's lid and Air Crisp for 2 minutes at 350 °F.
5. Transfer to a serving plate and enjoy.

Nutrition:

- InfoCalories: 141; Fat: 11g; Carbohydrates: 0.6g; Protein: 9g

Chicken Omelet

Servings: 2
Cooking Time: 16 Minutes
Ingredients:

- 1 teaspoon butter
- 1 small yellow onion, chopped
- ½ jalapeño pepper, seeded and chopped
- 3 eggs
- Black pepper and salt, as required
- ¼ cup cooked chicken, shredded

Directions:

1. Select the "Sauté/Sear" setting of Ninja Foodi and place the butter into the pot.
2. Press the "Start/Stop" button to initiate cooking and heat for about 2-3 minutes.
3. Add the onion and cook for about 4-5 minutes.
4. Add the jalapeño pepper and cook for about 1 minute.
5. Meanwhile, in a suitable, add the eggs, salt, and black pepper and beat well.
6. Press the "Start/Stop" button to pause cooking and stir in the chicken.
7. Top with the egg mixture evenly.
8. Close the Ninja Foodi's lid with a crisping lid and select "Air Crisp."
9. Set its cooking temperature to 355 °F for 5 minutes.
10. Press the "Start/Stop" button to initiate cooking.
11. Open the Ninja Foodi's lid and transfer the omelette onto a plate.
12. Cut into equal-sized wedges and serve hot.

Nutrition:

- InfoCalories: 153; Fat: 9.1g; Carbohydrates: 4g; Protein: 13.8g

Ham & Spinach Breakfast Bake

Servings: 6

Cooking Time: 30 Minutes

Ingredients:

- Nonstick cooking spray
- 10 eggs
- 1 cup spinach, chopped
- 1 cup ham, chopped
- 1 cup red peppers, chopped
- 1 cup onion, chopped
- 1 tsp garlic powder
- ½ tsp onion powder
- ¼ tsp salt
- ¼ tsp pepper
- 1 cup Swiss cheese, grated

Directions:

1. Select the bake function and heat cooker to 350°F. Spray the cooking pot with cooking spray.
2. In a large bowl, whisk eggs together.
3. Add remaining ingredients and mix well.
4. Pour into cooking pot and secure the tender-crisp lid. Cook 25-30 minutes, or until eggs are set and top has started to brown.
5. Let cool 5 minutes before serving.

Nutrition:

- InfoCalories 287,Total Fat 18g,Total Carbs 7g,Protein 23g,Sodium 629mg.

Pumpkin Coconut Breakfast Bake

Servings: 8

Cooking Time: 1 Hour 15 Minutes

Ingredients:

- Butter flavored cooking spray
- 5 eggs
- ½ cup coconut milk
- 2 cups pumpkin puree
- 1 banana, mashed
- 2 dates, pitted & chopped
- 1 tsp cinnamon
- 1 cup raspberries
- ¼ cup coconut, unsweetened & shredded

Directions:

1. Lightly spray an 8-inch baking dish with cooking spray.
2. In a large bowl, whisk together eggs and milk.
3. Whisk in pumpkin until combined.
4. Stir in banana, dates, and cinnamon. Pour into prepared dish.
5. Sprinkle berries over top.
6. Place the rack in the cooking pot and place the dish on it. Add the tender-crisp lid and select bake on 350°F. Bake 20 minutes.
7. Sprinkle coconut over the top and bake another 20-25 minutes until top is lightly browned and casserole is set. Slice and serve warm.

Nutrition:

- InfoCalories 113,Total Fat 5g,Total Carbs 14g,Protein 6g,Sodium 62mg.

Kale-egg Frittata

Servings: 6
Cooking Time: 20 Min
Ingredients:

- 1 ½ cups kale; chopped /195g
- 6 large eggs
- ¼ cup grated Parmesan cheese /32.5g
- 1 cup water /250ml
- 2 tbsp heavy cream /30ml
- ½ tsp freshly grated nutmeg /2.5g
- cooking spray
- Salt and black pepper to taste

Directions:

1. In a bowl, beat eggs, nutmeg, pepper, salt, and cream until smooth; stir in Parmesan cheese and kale. Apply a cooking spray to a cake pan. Wrap aluminum foil around outside of the pan to cover completely.
2. Place egg mixture into the prepared pan. Add water into the pot of your Foodi. Set your Foodi's reversible rack over the water. Gently lay the pan onto the reversible rack.
3. Seal the pressure lid, choose Pressure, set to High, and set the timer to 10 minutes. Press Start. When ready, release the pressure quickly.

Bacon & Egg Stuffed Squash

Servings: 4
Cooking Time: 30 Minutes
Ingredients:

- 1 large acorn squash
- 1 tbsp. olive oil
- ¼ tsp salt
- ¼ tsp pepper
- 4 eggs
- ¼ tsp thyme
- 2 slices turkey bacon, cook & crumble

Directions:

1. Select air fryer function and heat cooker to 425°F.
2. Cut the ends off the squash. Cut the squash, width-wise, into 4 equal slices and remove the seeds.
3. Brush both sides of the squash slices with oil and season with salt and pepper.
4. Place a sheet of parchment paper on the bottom of the cooker and place 2 slices of squash on it. Add the rack, another sheet of parchment paper and remaining slices of squash. Secure the tender-crisp lid and cook 15 minutes or until squash is tender.
5. Reduce heat to 350°F. Carefully remove the rack with the squash on it. Crack an egg in the middle of the bottom two squash slices. Replace the rack and crack an egg into the top two slices.
6. Close the tender-crisp lid and cook 12 minutes, or until eggs whites are cooked through. Sprinkle with thyme and bacon and serve immediately.

Nutrition:

- InfoCalories 156,Total Fat 10g,Total Carbs 12g,Protein 8g,Sodium 279mg.

Peanut Butter Banana Baked Oatmeal

Servings: 8
Cooking Time: 20 Minutes
Ingredients:

- Nonstick cooking spray
- 1 ½ cups oats
- 1/3 cup sugar
- ¾ cup almond milk, unsweetened
- 2 tbsp. coconut oil, melted
- 1 egg
- ½ cup peanut butter, no sugar added
- 1 tsp baking powder
- 1 tsp vanilla
- 1 banana, sliced

Directions:

1. Select bake function and heat to 350°F. Spray an 8-inch baking pan with cooking spray.
2. In a large bowl, combine all ingredients, except bananas, and mix until thoroughly combined. Pour into prepared pan in an even layer.
3. Layer the banana slices on the top and place in the cooker. Secure the tender-crisp lid and bake 20 minutes or until edges start to brown.
4. Carefully remove the pan from the cooker and let cool 10 minutes before slicing and serving.

Nutrition:

- InfoCalories 304,Total Fat 13g,Total Carbs 39g,Protein 11g,Sodium 118mg.

Breakfast Egg Pizza

Servings: 8
Cooking Time: 28 Minutes
Ingredients:

- 12 eggs
- 1/2 cup heavy cream
- 1/2 tsp salt
- 1/4 tsp pepper
- 8 oz sausage
- 2 cups peppers sliced
- 1 cup cheese shredded

Directions:

1. Heat peppers in a bowl for 3 minutes in the microwave.
2. Place air crisper basket in the Ninja Foodi and place the bacon in it.
3. Secure the Ninja Foodi lid and Air Fry them for 10 minutes.
4. Transfer the cooked crispy bacon to a plate and keep them aside.
5. Whisk eggs with salt, pepper, and cream in a bowl.
6. Pour this mixture in a greased baking pan.
7. Place the trivet in the Ninja Food cooking pot and set the baking pan over it.
8. Secure the Ninja Foodi lid and turn the pressure valve to 'closed' position.
9. Select 'Bake/Roast' for 15 minutes at 350 °F.
10. Once done, top the egg bake with cheese and peppers.
11. Broil this pizza for 3 minutes in the broiler until the cheese melts.
12. Serve warm.

Nutrition:

- InfoCalories 489; Total Fat 43.3g; Total Carbs 5g; Protein 22.2 g

Deviled Eggs(2)

Servings: 6
Cooking Time: 20 Min
Ingredients:

- 10 large eggs
- ¼ cup cream cheese /32.5ml
- ¼ cup mayonnaise /62.5ml
- 1 cup water /250ml
- ¼ tsp chili powder /1.25g
- salt and ground black pepper to taste

Directions:

1. Add water to the Foodi's pot. Insert the eggs into the steamer basket; place into the pot. Seal the pressure lid, choose Pressure, set to High, and set the timer to 5 minutes. Press Start.When ready, release the pressure quickly.
2. Drop eggs into an ice bath to cool for 5 minutes. Press Start. Peel eggs and halve them.
3. Transfer yolks to a bowl and use a fork to mash; stir in cream cheese, and mayonnaise. Add pepper and salt for seasoning. Ladle yolk mixture into egg white halves.

Bacon And Sausage Cheesecake

Servings: 6
Cooking Time: 25 Min
Ingredients:

- 8 eggs, cracked into a bowl
- 8 oz. breakfast sau sage; chopped /240g
- 4 slices bread, cut into ½ -inch cubes
- 1 large green bell pepper; chopped
- 1 large red bell pepper; chopped
- 1 cup chopped green onion /130g
- ½ cup milk /125ml
- 2 cups water /500ml
- 1 cup grated Cheddar cheese /130g
- 3 bacon slices; chopped
- 1 tsp red chili flakes /5g
- Salt and black pepper to taste

Directions:

1. Add the eggs, sausage chorizo, bacon slices, green and red bell peppers, green onion, chili flakes, cheddar cheese, salt, pepper, and milk to a bowl and use a whisk to beat them together.
2. Grease a bundt pan with cooking spray and pour the egg mixture into it. After, drop the bread slices in the egg mixture all around while using a spoon to push them into the mixture.
3. Open the Ninja Foodi, pour in water, and fit the rack at the center of the pot. Place bundt pan on the rack and seal the pressure lid. Select Pressure mode on High pressure for 6 minutes, and press Start/Stop.
4. Once the timer goes off, press Start/Stop, do a quick pressure release. Run a knife around the egg in the bundt pan, close the crisping lid and cook for another 4 minutes on Bake/Roast on 380 °F or 194°C.
5. When ready, place a serving plate on the bundt pan, and then, turn the egg bundt over. Use a knife to cut the egg into slices. Serve with a sauce of your choice.

Chapter 2 Vegan & Vegetable

Veggie Primavera

Servings: 6
Cooking Time: 25 Minutes

Ingredients:

- 2 tbsp. olive oil
- 1 tsp Italian seasoning
- 1 tsp garlic powder
- ½ tsp salt
- ½ tsp pepper

- 12 oz. baby red potatoes, quartered
- 2 ears corn, husked & cut into 1-inch rounds
- 4 oz. baby carrots
- ½ red onion, cut in wedges
- 4 oz. fresh sugar snap peas

Directions:

1. In a large bowl, combine oil, Italian seasoning, garlic powder, salt, and pepper, mix well.
2. Add remaining ingredients, except peas, and toss to coat the vegetables.
3. Spray the cooking pot with cooking spray and add the vegetable mixture.
4. Add the tender-crisp lid and set to roast on 425°F. Roast vegetables 15 minutes, turning halfway through cooking time.
5. Add the peas and stir to mix. Roast another 10-15 minutes until vegetables are lightly browned and tender. Serve immediately.

Nutrition:

- InfoCalories 142,Total Fat 5g,Total Carbs 23g,Protein 3g,Sodium 222mg.

Spicy Cabbage Soup

Servings: 6
Cooking Time: 20 Minutes

Ingredients:

- Nonstick cooking spray
- 2 cups onion, chopped fine
- 14 oz. tomatoes with green chilies
- 8 oz. tomato sauce

- 1 tsp garlic powder
- 4 cups water
- 3 cups green cabbage, shredded
- 1 tbsp. brown sugar

Directions:

1. Spray the cooking pot with cooking spray and set to sauté on med-high heat.
2. Add onions and cook until tender, stirring occasionally, about 3-4 minutes.
3. Add tomatoes with chilies to a blender and process about 30 seconds until pureed.
4. Stir the pureed tomatoes, tomato sauce, garlic, and water into the onions until combined.
5. Add the lid and set to pressure cook on high. Set timer for 6 minutes. When timer goes off, use natural release to remove the pressure.
6. Stir in cabbage and brown sugar. Recover and set to pressure cook on high. Set timer for 8 minutes. When timer goes off, use natural release again. Stir well and serve.

Nutrition:

- InfoCalories 56,Total Fat 0g,Total Carbs 13g,Protein 2g,Sodium 283mg.

Pumpkin Soup

Servings: 8
Cooking Time: 8 Hours
Ingredients:

- 15 oz. pumpkin
- 1 cup celery, chopped
- ½ cup carrots, chopped fine
- ½ cup onion, chopped fine
- ¼ tsp salt
- ½ tsp oregano
- ½ tsp rosemary
- ¼ tsp red pepper
- ¼ tsp ginger
- 28 oz. vegetable broth
- ¼ cup whipped cream
- 3 tbsp. pumpkin seeds, toasted

Directions:

1. Add all ingredients, except whipped cream and pumpkin seeds, to the cooking pot, mix well.
2. Add the lid and set to slow cook on low. Cook 6-8 hours.
3. Stir in whipped cream until thoroughly combined. Ladle into bowls and top with pumpkin seeds. Serve.

Nutrition:

- InfoCalories 78,Total Fat 5g,Total Carbs 8g,Protein 3g,Sodium 500mg.

Italian Sausage With Garlic Mash

Servings: 6
Cooking Time: 30 Min
Ingredients:

- 6 Italian sausages
- 4 large potatoes, peeled and cut into 1½-inch chunks
- 2 garlic cloves, smashed
- ⅓ cup butter, melted /44ml
- ¼ cup milk; at room temperature, or more as needed /62.5ml
- 1 ½ cups water /375ml
- 1 tbsp olive oil /15ml
- 1 tbsp chopped chives/15g
- salt and ground black pepper to taste

Directions:

1. Select Sear/Sauté, set to Medium High, and choose Start/Stop to preheat the pot and heat olive oil. Cook for 8-10 minutes, turning periodically until browned. Set aside. Wipe the pot with paper towels. Add in water and set the reversible rack over water. Place potatoes onto the reversible rack.
2. Seal the pressure lid, choose Pressure, set to High, and set the timer to 12 minutes. Press Start.
3. When ready, release the pressure quickly. Remove reversible rack from the pot. Drain water from the pot. Return potatoes to pot. Add in salt, butter, pepper, garlic, and milk and use a hand masher to mash until no large lumps remain.
4. Using an immersion blender, blend potatoes on Low for 1 minute until fluffy and light. Avoid over-blending to ensure the potatoes do not become gluey!
5. Transfer the mash to a serving plate, top with sausages and scatter chopped chives over to serve.

Tofu & Carrot Toss

Servings: 4

Cooking Time: 20 Minutes

Ingredients:

- 1 tbsp. coconut oil
- 1 lb. carrots, grated
- 1 lb. extra firm tofu, drained, pressed & crumbled
- 1/3 cup soy sauce
- 1/3 cup sesame seeds
- 1 tsp dark sesame oil
- 1/4 cup cilantro, chopped

Directions:

1. Add oil to the cooking pot and set to sauté on med-high heat.
2. Add carrots and cook 15 minutes, stirring occasionally.
3. Add tofu and cook until carrots are tender, about 5 minutes. Stir in soy sauce and sesame seeds and cook 1 minute more, stirring constantly.
4. Turn the heat off and stir in sesame oil and cilantro. Serve over rice.

Nutrition:

- InfoCalories 279,Total Fat 20g,Total Carbs 16g,Protein 17g,Sodium 851mg.

Caprese Pasta Salad

Servings:8

Cooking Time: 3 Minutes

Ingredients:

- 1 box elbow pasta
- 4 cups water
- 1 tablespoon sea salt
- 2 tablespoons extra-virgin olive oil
- ½ cup red bell pepper, diced
- 1 cup cherry tomatoes, sliced
- ¼ cup black olives, sliced
- ½ pound fresh mozzarella, diced
- ½ cup chopped fresh basil
- ½ cup Italian dressing

Directions:

1. Place the pasta, water, and salt in the pot. Assemble pressure lid, making sure the pressure release valve is in the SEAL position.
2. Select PRESSURE and set to HI. Set time to 3 minutes. Select START/STOP to begin.
3. When pressure cooking is complete, allow pressure to naturally release for 10 minutes. After 10 minutes, quick release remaining pressure by moving the pressure release valve to the VENT position. Carefully remove lid when unit has finished releasing pressure.
4. Drain the pasta in a colander. Place the pasta in a large bowl and toss with the olive oil. Set aside to cool for 20 minutes.
5. Stir in the bell pepper, cherry tomatoes, olives, mozzarella, and basil. Gently fold in the Italian seasoning.
6. Serve immediately or cover and refrigerate for later.

Nutrition:

- InfoCalories: 377,Total Fat: 15g,Sodium: 694mg,Carbohydrates: 45g,Protein: 14g.

Zucchini Quinoa Stuffed Red Peppers

Servings: 4

Cooking Time: 40 Min

Ingredients:

- 1 small zucchini; chopped
- 4 red bell peppers
- 2 large tomatoes; chopped
- 1 small onion; chopped
- 2 cloves garlic, minced
- 1 cup quinoa, rinsed /130g
- 1 cup grated Gouda cheese /130g
- ½ cup chopped mushrooms /65g
- 1 ½ cup water /375ml
- 2 cups chicken broth /500ml
- 1 tbsp olive oil /15ml
- ½ tsp smoked paprika /2.5g
- Salt and black pepper to taste

Directions:

1. Select Sear/Sauté mode on High. Once it is ready, add the olive oil to heat and then add the onion and garlic. Sauté for 3 minutes to soften, stirring occasionally.

2. Include the tomatoes, cook for 3 minutes and then add the quinoa, zucchinis, and mushrooms. Season with paprika, salt, and black pepper and stir with a spoon. Cook for 5 to 7 minutes, then, turn the pot off.

3. Use a knife to cut the bell peppers in halves (lengthwise) and remove their seeds and stems.

4. Spoon the quinoa mixture into the bell peppers. Put the peppers in a greased baking dish and pour the broth over.

5. Wipe the pot clean with some paper towels, and pour the water into it. After, fit the steamer rack at the bottom of the pot.

6. Place the baking dish on top of the reversible rack, cover with aluminum foil, close the lid, secure the pressure valve, and select Pressure mode on High pressure for 15 minutes. Press Start/Stop.

7. Once the timer has ended, do a quick pressure release and open the lid. Remove the aluminum foil and sprinkle with the gouda cheese.

8. Close the crisping lid, select Bake/Roast mode and cook for 10 minutes on 375 °F or 191°C. Arrange the stuffed peppers on a serving platter and serve right away or as a side to a meat dish.

Mushroom Leek Soup With Parmesan Croutons

Servings: 4

Cooking Time: 15 Minutes

Ingredients:

- 4 slices brioche bread, cut in ¼-inch cubes
- 2 tbsp. olive oil
- 2 tbsp. parmesan cheese
- 2 tsp pepper
- 3 tbsp. butter
- 4 leeks, trimmed, sliced ½-inch thick
- 4 cups cremini mushrooms, sliced
- ½ cup white wine
- 3 tbsp. flour
- 4 cups chicken broth, low sodium
- 2/3 cup milk
- ½ tsp salt

Directions:

1. In a large bowl, combine bread, olive oil, parmesan, and pepper, toss to coat bread.
2. Set cooker to sauté on medium heat. Add the bread and cook, stirring frequently, until toasted, about 5 minutes. Transfer to a plate.
3. Add the butter to the cooking pot and let it melt. Add the leeks and cook 5 minutes or until translucent. Add the mushrooms and cook another 5 minutes.
4. Stir in wine scraping up any browned bits on the bottom of the pan. Cook just until liquid is almost evaporated then stir in flour for 1 minute.
5. Add the broth, stirring until no lumps remain. Add the milk and salt and let simmer 5 minutes.
6. Use an immersion blender, or transfer to a blender, and process until almost smooth. Ladle into bowls and top with croutons. Serve.

Nutrition:

- InfoCalories 94,Total Fat 5g,Total Carbs 8g,Protein 3g,Sodium 61mg.

Zucchini Cream Soup

Servings: 6
Cooking Time: 40 Minutes
Ingredients:

- Nonstick cooking spray
- 1 cup onion, chopped
- ½ red bell pepper, chopped
- 3 cloves garlic, chopped fine
- 1 ½ lb. zucchini, cut in ½-inch cubes
- 28 oz. vegetable broth, low sodium
- 1 tbsp. fresh dill, chopped
- ½ tsp salt
- ¼ tsp pepper
- 1 cup skim milk
- 3 tbsp. cornstarch

Directions:

1. Spray the cooking pot with cooking spray. Set to sauté on med-high heat.
2. Add onion, bell pepper, and garlic and cook 4-5 minutes, stirring frequently, until soft.
3. Add zucchini, broth, dill, salt, and pepper and bring to a boil. Reduce heat to low, cover and cook 25-30 minutes until zucchini is soft.
4. In a small bowl, whisk together milk and cornstarch until smooth. Stir into soup and cook another 2-3 minutes until thickened. Serve.

Nutrition:

- InfoCalories 72,Total Fat 1g,Total Carbs 14g,Protein 5g,Sodium 764mg.

Asparagus With Feta

Servings: 4
Cooking Time: 15 Min
Ingredients:

- 1-pound asparagus spears, ends trimmed /450g
- 1 lemon, cut into wedges
- 1 cup feta cheese; cubed /130g
- 1 cup water /250ml
- 1 tbsp olive oil /15ml
- salt and freshly ground black pepper to taste

Directions:

1. Into the pot, add water and set trivet over the water. Place steamer basket on the trivet. Place the asparagus into the steamer basket. Seal the pressure lid, choose Pressure, set to High, and set the timer to 1 minute. Press Start.
2. When ready, release the pressure quickly. Add olive oil in a bowl and toss in asparagus until well coated; season with pepper and salt. Serve alongside feta cheese and lemon wedges.

Quick Indian-style Curry

Servings:8

Cooking Time: 35 Minutes

Ingredients:

- 1 tablespoon vegetable oil
- 1 small onion, diced
- 1 small bell pepper, diced
- 1 large potato, cut into 1-inch cubes
- 1 teaspoon ground turmeric
- 1 teaspoon cumin seeds
- 1 teaspoon ground cumin
- 1 teaspoon garam masala (optional)
- 1 teaspoon curry powder
- 1 jar curry sauce, plus 1 jar water
- 1 can diced tomatoes
- 1 cup dried red lentils
- 8 ounces paneer, cubed (optional)
- 1 cup fresh cilantro, roughly chopped (optional)
- Salt
- Freshly ground black pepper

Directions:

1. Select SEAR/SAUTÉ and set temperature to HI. Select START/STOP to begin and allow to preheat for 5 minutes.
2. Add the oil to the pot and allow to heat for 1 minute. Add the onion and bell pepper and sauté for 3 to 4 minutes.
3. Add the potato, turmeric, cumin seeds, cumin, garam masala, and curry powder. Stir and cook for 5 minutes.
4. Stir in the curry sauce, water, tomatoes, and lentils.
5. Assemble the pressure lid, making sure the pressure release valve is in the SEAL position.
6. Select PRESSURE and set to HI. Set the time to 15 minutes. Select START/STOP to begin.
7. When pressure cooking is complete, allow the pressure to naturally release for 10 minutes. After 10 minutes, quick release any remaining pressure by moving the pressure release valve to the VENT position. Carefully remove the lid when the unit has finished releasing pressure.
8. Stir in the paneer (if using) and cilantro. Taste and season with salt and pepper, as needed.

Nutrition:

- InfoCalories: 217,Total Fat: 6g,Sodium: 27mg,Carbohydrates: 33g,Protein: 8g.

Spinach Gratin & Eggs

Servings: 6
Cooking Time: 1 Hour
Ingredients:

- 3 lbs. fresh spinach, blanched & drained well
- 2 cups milk
- 2 tbsp. butter
- 2 tbsp. flour
- ¾ tsp nutmeg
- 1/8 tsp pepper
- ¼ cup Gruyere cheese, grated
- 6 eggs, hard boiled & cut in half
- 4 tbsp. seasoned bread crumbs
- 1 tbsp. extra virgin olive oil

Directions:

1. Chop the spinach and place in a large bowl, Season with salt and pepper.
2. In a small saucepan, over medium heat, heat milk until steamy.
3. Add butter to the cooking pot and set to sauté on medium heat.
4. Once butter has melted, whisk in flour until smooth, cook, whisking 1-2 minutes. Slowly whisk in the hot milk and continue whisking until no lumps remain. Add nutmeg and pepper and cook until thickened, about 1-2 minutes.
5. Add the spinach and mix well. Sprinkle the Gruyere over the top. Arrange the eggs, cut side up, on the top of the spinach, press lightly so the eggs are even with the top of the spinach.
6. Sprinkle the bread crumbs over the top and drizzle with olive oil. Add the tender-crisp lid and set to bake on 375°F. Bake 25-30 minutes until top is nicely browned and casserole is heated through. Serve.

Nutrition:

- InfoCalories 74,Total Fat 4g,Total Carbs 5g,Protein 5g,Sodium 90mg.

Southern Pineapple Casserole

Servings: 8
Cooking Time: 35 Minutes
Ingredients:

- Nonstick cooking spray
- 1/3 cup butter, soft
- 1/4 cup Stevia
- 2 eggs
- 2 egg whites
- 1 tsp vanilla
- 2 tbsp. flour
- 20 oz. crushed pineapple in juice, drained; reserve 1 cup liquid
- 5 slices whole-wheat bread, cubed

Directions:

1. Spray the cooking pot with cooking spray.
2. In a large bowl, beat butter and Stevia until smooth and creamy.
3. Beat in eggs, egg whites, and vanilla until combined.
4. Stir in flour, pineapple, and reserved juice and mix well.
5. Add bread and toss to coat. Pour into cooking pot.
6. Add tender-crisp lid and set to bake on 350°F. Bake 30-35 minutes or until a knife inserted in center comes out clean. Serve warm.

Nutrition:

- InfoCalories 191,Total Fat 10g,Total Carbs 29g,Protein 5g,Sodium 183mg.

Beets And Carrots

Servings: 4

Cooking Time: 20 Minutes

Ingredients:

- 1-pound beets, peeled and roughly cubed
- 1-pound baby carrots, peeled
- Black pepper and salt to the taste
- 2 tablespoons olive oil
- 1 tablespoon chives, minced

Directions:

1. In a suitable, mix the beets with the carrots and the other ingredients and toss.
2. Put the beets and carrots in the Foodi's basket.
3. Cook on Air Crisp at 390 °F for 20 minutes, divide between plates and serve.

Nutrition:

- InfoCalories: 150; Fat: 4.5g; Carbohydrates: 7.3g; Protein: 3.6g

Vegan Stuffed Peppers

Servings: 4

Cooking Time: 35 Minutes

Ingredients:

- Nonstick cooking spray
- 2 bell peppers, halved lengthwise & cleaned
- 2 tbsp. olive oil
- ½ cup onion, chopped
- 4 cloves garlic, chopped fine
- 2 tomatoes, chopped fine
- ¼ tsp salt
- ¼ cup fresh parsley, chopped
- 1/3 cup dry bread crumbs
- 2 tbsp. dry white wine
- ¼ tsp pepper
- 2 tbsp. parmesan cheese

Directions:

1. Spray an 8x8-inch baking dish with cooking spray.
2. Fill the cooking pot halfway full with water. Set to sauté on high heat and bring to a boil.
3. Add the pepper halves and boil 4-5 minutes or until they start to soften. Drain and place peppers in cold water. Drain again.
4. Add oil to the cooking pot and set to medium heat. Add onion and garlic and cook just until onion has softened. Turn off heat and stir in remaining ingredients, except pepper and parmesan cheese, mix well.
5. Spoon the onion mixture into the peppers and place them in prepared dish. Sprinkle with parmesan cheese.
6. Place the rack in the cooking pot and add the peppers. Add the tender-crisp lid and set to bake on 350°F. Bake 35-40 minutes until filling is hot and peppers are tender. Serve immediately.

Nutrition:

- InfoCalories 152,Total Fat 8g,Total Carbs 17g,Protein 4g,Sodium 285mg.

Mushroom Goulash

Servings: 6
Cooking Time: 40 Minutes
Ingredients:

- 2 tbsp. olive oil, divided
- ½ onion, sliced thin
- 1 red bell pepper, chopped
- 2 lbs. mushrooms, chopped
- ½ tsp salt
- ¼ tsp pepper

- 14 oz. tomatoes, diced
- 2 cups vegetable broth, low sodium
- 1 tsp garlic powder
- 1 ½ tbsp. paprika
- 5 -6 sprigs fresh thyme

Directions:

1. Add half the oil to the cooking pot and set to sauté on med-high.
2. Add the onion and cook until they start to get soft, about 4 minutes. Add the red pepper and cook 3-5 minutes or until onions start to caramelize. Transfer to a plate.
3. Add the remaining oil to the pot and let it get hot. Add the mushrooms and cook until liquid is almost evaporated, stirring occasionally. Season with salt and pepper.
4. Add the peppers and onions back to the pot along with tomatoes, broth, garlic powder, paprika, and thyme, stir to mix well. Bring to a boil, cover, reduce heat to med-low and let simmer 20 minutes. Serve.

Nutrition:

- InfoCalories 115,Total Fat 5g,Total Carbs 14g,Protein 6g,Sodium 544mg.

Artichoke Lasagna Rolls

Servings: 10
Cooking Time: 55 Minutes
Ingredients:

- 2 tsp olive oil
- ½ cup onion, chopped fine
- 24 oz. tomato and basil pasta sauce
- 1 cup ricotta cheese, low fat
- 1 egg

- 3 cloves garlic, chopped fine
- 14 oz. artichoke hearts, drained, quartered
- 2 tbsp. fresh basil, chopped
- 2 tbsp. parmesan cheese
- 10 lasagna noodles, cooked & drained

Directions:

1. Add oil to the cooking pot and set to sauté on med-high heat.
2. Add the onion and cook 5 minutes until soft. Stir in tomato sauce and cook another 5 minutes. Transfer all but 1 cup of the sauce to a bowl.
3. In a large bowl, combine ricotta cheese, egg, garlic, artichokes, basil, and parmesan cheese, mix well.
4. Lay lasagna noodles on a work surface and spoon cheese mixture over noodles. Roll up tightly and stand up in the cooking pot.
5. Pour remaining sauce over the top. Add the tender-crisp lid and set to bake on 350°F. Bake 40-45 minutes. Serve.

Nutrition:

- InfoCalories 172,Total Fat 6g,Total Carbs 23g,Protein 8g,Sodium 330mg.

Corn & Black Bean Chili

Servings: 6
Cooking Time: 15 Minutes
Ingredients:

- 2 ½ cups black beans, rinsed & sorted
- 6 ½ cups water
- 4 cloves garlic, chopped fine
- 1 red bell pepper, chopped
- 1 green bell pepper, chopped
- 2 chilies in adobo sauce, chopped
- 1 red onion, chopped
- 14 oz. tomatoes, diced
- 1 tbsp. salt
- 2 tbsp. chili powder
- 1 tbsp. ground cumin
- 1 tbsp. tomato paste
- 2 cups water
- 2 cups corn

Directions:

1. Add beans and water to the cooking pot. Add the lid and set to pressure cook on high. Set the timer for 8 minutes. Once timer goes off, use quick release to remove the pressure. Drain beans and return to pot.
2. Add remaining ingredients, except the corn, and stir to mix. Recover and pressure cook on high. Set the timer for 4 minutes. Once the timer goes off, use quick release to remove the pressure again.
3. Stir in the corn and pressure cook another 2-3 minutes. Stir well and serve.

Nutrition:

- InfoCalories 337,Total Fat 3g,Total Carbs 64g,Protein 20g,Sodium 1728mg.

Peanut Tofu & Noodles

Servings: 4
Cooking Time: 10 Minutes
Ingredients:

- Nonstick cooking spray
- 16 oz. firm tofu, cubed
- ½ lb. linguine
- 2 cups broccoli, chopped
- ¼ cup peanut butter
- ¼ cup soy sauce, low sodium
- 2 tbsp. rice vinegar
- 2 tbsp. peanuts, chopped

Directions:

1. Spray the fryer basket with cooking spray.
2. Place tofu in the basket and add the tender-crisp lid. Set to air fry on 400°F. Cook tofu 10 minutes, turning over halfway through cooking time.
3. Prepare pasta according to package directions. Add the broccoli during the last 5 minutes of cooking time. Drain.
4. In a small bowl, whisk together peanut butter, soy sauce, and vinegar until smooth.
5. Add the tofu and sauce to the pasta and toss until evenly distributed. Ladle onto serving plates and top with peanuts. Serve immediately.

Nutrition:

- InfoCalories 380,Total Fat 19g,Total Carbs 31g,Protein 30g,Sodium 705mg.

Whole Roasted Broccoli And White Beans With Harissa, Tahini, And Lemon

Servings:4

Cooking Time: 30 Minutes

Ingredients:

- 2 cups water
- 2 small heads broccoli, cut in half
- 2 tablespoons unsalted butter
- ½ white onion, minced
- 2 garlic cloves, minced
- 1 can cannellini beans, rinsed and drained
- 1 can fire-roasted tomatoes and peppers
- 1 tablespoon spicy harissa
- Sea salt
- Freshly ground black pepper
- ¼ cup tahini
- ¼ cup walnuts, toasted and chopped
- Zest of 1 lemon
- Juice of 1 lemon

Directions:

1. Place Reversible Rack in pot, making sure it is in the lowest position. Pour the water into the pot and place the broccoli on the rack. Assemble the pressure lid, making sure the pressure release valve is in the SEAL position.

2. Select STEAM. Set time to 8 minutes. Select START/STOP to begin.

3. When steaming is complete, quick release the pressure by turning the pressure release valve to the VENT position. Carefully remove lid when unit has finished releasing pressure.

4. Remove rack and broccoli and set aside. Drain the remaining water from the pot and reinsert it in base.

5. Select SEAR/SAUTÉ and set to HI. Select START/STOP to begin. Let preheat for 5 minutes.

6. Add the butter to pot. Once melted, add the onions and garlic and cook for 3 minutes. Add the beans, tomatoes, harissa, and season with salt and pepper. Cook for 4 minutes.

7. Reinsert rack and broccoli. Close crisping lid.

8. Select AIR CRISP, set temperature to 390°F, and set time to 15 minutes. Select START/STOP to begin.

9. After 10 minutes, open lid and flip the broccoli. Close lid and continue cooking.

10. When cooking is complete, remove rack with broccoli from pot. Place the beans in serving dishes and top with the broccoli. Drizzle tahini over the broccoli and sprinkle with walnuts. Garnish with the lemon zest and juice and serve.

Nutrition:

- InfoCalories: 426,Total Fat: 25g,Sodium: 435mg,Carbohydrates: 39g,Protein: 15g.

Chapter 3 Poultry

Chicken With Roasted Red Pepper Sauce

Servings: 4

Cooking Time: 23 Min

Ingredients:

- 4 chicken breasts; skinless and boneless
- ¼ cup roasted red peppers; chopped /32.5g
- ½ cup chicken broth /125ml
- ½ cup heavy cream /125ml
- 1 tbsp basil pesto /15g
- 1 tbsp cornstarch /15g
- ⅓ tsp Italian Seasoning /1.67g
- ⅓ tsp minced garlic /1.67g
- Salt and black pepper to taste

Directions:

1. In the inner pot of the Foodi, add the chicken at the bottom. Pour the chicken broth and add Italian seasoning, garlic, salt, and pepper.
2. Close the pressure lid, secure the pressure valve, and select Pressure mode on High for 15 minutes. Press Start/Stop.
3. Once the timer has ended, do a natural pressure release for 5 minutes and open the lid. Use a spoon to remove the chicken onto a plate. Scoop out any fat or unwanted chunks from the sauce.
4. In a small bowl, add the cream, cornstarch, red peppers, and pesto. Mix them with a spoon. Pour the creamy mixture into the pot and close the crisping lid.
5. Select Broil mode and cook for 4 minutes. Serve the chicken with sauce over on a bed of cooked quinoa.

Chicken & Black Bean Chowder

Servings: 6

Cooking Time: 6 Hours

Ingredients:

- 15 oz. black beans, rinsed & drained
- 3 chicken breasts, boneless & skinless
- 1 cup corn, frozen
- 16 oz. salsa
- 4 cups chicken broth, low sodium
- 4 oz. green chilies, diced
- ¼ cup cilantro, chopped
- 1 lime, cut in wedges

Directions:

1. Place all ingredients, except cilantro and limes, in the cooking pot, stir to mix well.
2. Add the lid and set to slow cook on low. Cook 5-6 hours until chicken is tender.
3. Transfer chicken to a cutting board and shred. Return to the pot and increase temperature to high. Cook 30 minutes.
4. Ladle into bowls and serve garnished with cilantro and a lime wedge.

Nutrition:

- InfoCalories 350,Total Fat 8g,Total Carbs 29g,Protein 42g,Sodium 749mg.

Apple Butter Chicken

Servings: 4

Cooking Time: 35 Minutes

Ingredients:

- Nonstick cooking spray
- 4 chicken breast halves, boneless & skinless
- ½ tsp salt
- 1/8 tsp pepper
- ½ cup apple butter
- ¼ cup cheddar cheese, grated

Directions:

1. Spray cooking pot with cooking spray.
2. Place chicken in the pot and season with salt and pepper. Spread apple butter evenly over the chicken.
3. Add the tender-crisp lid and set to bake on 350°F. Bake 25-30 minutes until chicken is cooked through.
4. Open the lid and sprinkle the cheese over the chicken. Close the lid and bake another 3-5 minutes until cheese is melted. Serve.

Nutrition:

- InfoCalories 344,Total Fat 7g,Total Carbs 28g,Protein 40g,Sodium 426mg.

Turkey Meatballs

Servings: 4

Cooking Time: 4 Minutes

Ingredients:

- 1-pound ground turkey
- 1 cup onion, shredded
- 1/4 cup heavy whip cream
- 2 teaspoon salt
- 1 cup carrots, shredded
- 1/2 teaspoon ground caraway seeds
- 1 and 1/2 teaspoons black pepper
- 1/4 teaspoon ground allspice
- 1 cup almond meal
- 1/2 cup almond milk
- 2 tablespoons unsalted butter

Directions:

1. Transfer meat to a suitable.
2. Add cream, almond meal, onion, carrot, 1 teaspoon salt, caraway, 1/2 teaspoon pepper, allspice, and mix well.
3. Refrigerate the mixture for 30 minutes.
4. Once the mixture is cooled, use your hands to scoop the mixture into meatballs.
5. Place the turkey balls in your Ninja Foodi pot.
6. Add milk, pats of butter and sprinkle 1 teaspoon salt, 1 teaspoon black pepper.
7. Lock and secure the Ninja Foodi's lid, then cook on "HIGH" pressure for 4 minutes.
8. Quick-release pressure.
9. Unlock and secure the Ninja Foodi's lid and serve.
10. Enjoy.

Nutrition:

- InfoCalories: 338; Fat: 23g; Carbohydrates: 7g; Protein: 23g

Cajun Turkey Breast

Servings:8
Cooking Time: 35 Minutes
Ingredients:

- 1 boneless, skinless turkey breast
- 2 tablespoons Cajun spice seasoning
- 1 tablespoon kosher salt
- ½ cup water

Directions:

1. Season turkey breast liberally, evenly, and on all sides with the Cajun spice seasoning and salt.
2. Pour the water into the pot. Place the Cook & Crisp Basket in the pot, then place the turkey into the basket. Assemble pressure lid, making sure the pressure release valve is in the SEAL position.
3. Select PRESSURE and set to HI. Set time to 20 minutes. Select START/STOP to begin.
4. When pressure cooking is complete, quick release the pressure by moving the pressure release valve to the VENT position. Carefully remove lid when unit has finished releasing pressure.
5. Close crisping lid. Select AIR CRISP, set temperature to 360°F, and set time to 15 minutes. Select START/STOP to begin.
6. When cooking is complete, open lid and transfer the turkey breast to a cutting board. Let rest for at least 10 minutes before slicing or serving.

Nutrition:

- InfoCalories: 229,Total Fat: 1g,Sodium: 230mg,Carbohydrates: 0g,Protein: 54g.

Turkey And Brown Rice Salad With Peanuts

Servings: 4
Cooking Time: 60 Min
Ingredients:

- 1 pound turkey tenderloins /450g
- 3 celery stalks, thinly sliced
- 1 apple, cored and cubed
- 1 cup brown rice /130g
- ½ cup peanuts, toasted /65g
- 4 cups water /1000ml
- A pinch of sugar
- 3 tbsp apple cider vinegar /45ml
- ⅛ tsp freshly ground black pepper /0.625g
- ¼ tsp celery seeds /1.25g
- 2¼ tsp salt /11.25g
- 3 tsp peanut oil; divided /15ml

Directions:

1. Pour the water into the inner pot. Stir in the brown rice and 1 tsp or 5g of salt. Lock the pressure lid into the Seal position. Choose Pressure; adjust the pressure to High and the cook time to 10 minutes. Press Start.
2. Season the turkey on both sides with salt; set aside. After cooking the brown rice, perform a natural pressure release for 10 minutes. Carefully open the lid and spoon the rice into a large bowl to cool completely.
3. Put the turkey in the Crisping Basket and brush with 2 tsp s of peanut oil. Fix in the basket. Close the crisping lid and Choose Bake/Roast; adjust the temperature to 375°F or 191°C and the cook time to 12 minutes; press Start.
4. Pour the remaining peanut oil and the vinegar into a jar with a tight-fitting lid. Add the black pepper, celery seeds, salt, and sugar.
5. Close the jar and shake until the ingredients properly combined. When the turkey is ready, transfer to a plate to cool for several minutes. Cut it into bite-size chunks and add to the rice along with the peanuts, celery, and apple.
6. Pour half the dressing over the salad and toss gently to coat, adding more dressing as desired. Proceed to serve the salad.

Chicken Cacciatore

Servings: 4
Cooking Time: 40 Min
Ingredients:

- 1 pound chicken drumsticks, boneless, skinless /450g
- ½ cup dry red wine /125ml
- ¾ cup chicken stock /188ml
- 1 cup black olives, pitted and sliced /130g
- 2 bay leaves
- 1 pinch red pepper flakes
- 1 can diced tomatoes /840g
- 1carrot; chopped
- 1 red bell pepper; chopped
- 1 yellow bell pepper; chopped
- 1 onion; chopped
- 4 garlic cloves, thinly sliced
- 2 tsp olive oil /10ml
- 1 tsp dried basil /5g
- 1 tsp dried parsley /5g
- 2 tsp dried oregano /10g
- 1½ tsp freshly ground black pepper /7.5g
- 2 tsp salt /10g

Directions:

1. Warm oil on Sear/Sauté. Add pepper and salt to the chicken drumsticks. In batches, sear the chicken for 5-6 minutes until golden-brown. Set aside on a plate. Drain the cooker and remain with 1 tbsp of fat.
2. In the hot oil, sauté onion, garlic, and bell peppers for 4 minutes until softened; add red pepper flakes, basil, parsley, and oregano, and cook for 30 more seconds. Season with salt and pepper.
3. Stir in tomatoes, olives, chicken stock, red wine and bay leaves.
4. Return chicken to the pot. Seal the pressure lid, choose Pressure, set to High, and set the timer to 15 minutes. Press Start.
5. When ready, release the pressure quickly. Divide chicken between four serving bowls; top with tomato mixture before serving.

Sticky Orange Chicken

Servings: 4
Cooking Time: 30 Min
Ingredients:

- 2 chicken breasts; cubed
- 1 cup diced orange /130g
- ⅓ cup soy sauce /188ml
- ⅓ cup chicken stock /188ml
- ⅓ cup hoisin sauce /188ml
- 3 cups hot cooked quinoa /390g
- ½ cup honey /125ml
- ½ cup orange juice /125ml
- 1 garlic clove; minced
- 2 tsp cornstarch /10g
- 2 tsp water /10ml

Directions:

1. Arrange the chicken to the bottom of the Foodi's pot. In a bowl, mix honey, soy sauce, garlic, hoisin sauce, chicken stock, and orange juice, until the honey is dissolved; pour the mixture over the chicken.
2. Seal the pressure lid, choose Pressure, set to High, and set the timer to 7 minutes. Press Start. When ready, release the pressure quickly. Take the chicken from the pot and set to a bowl. Press Sear/Sauté.
3. In a small bowl, mix water with cornstarch; pour into the liquid within the pot and cook for 3 minutes until thick. Stir diced orange and chicken into the sauce until well coated. Serve with quinoa.

Bacon & Cranberry Stuffed Turkey Breast

Servings: 4

Cooking Time: 1 Hour

Ingredients:

- ¼ oz. porcini mushrooms, dried
- 1 slice bacon, thick cut, chopped
- ¼ cup shallot, chopped fine
- 2 tbsp. cranberries, dried, chopped
- 1 tsp fresh sage, chopped fine
- ½ cup bread crumbs
- 1 tbsp. fresh parsley, chopped
- 3 tbsp. chicken broth, low sodium
- 2 lb. turkey breast, boneless
- 2 tbsp. butter, soft
- ½ tsp salt

Directions:

1. In a small bowl, add the mushrooms and enough hot water to cover them. Let sit 15 minutes, then drain and chop them.
2. Set the cooker to sauté on medium heat. Add the bacon and cook until crisp. Transfer to a paper-towel lined plate.
3. Add the shallots and cook until they start to brown, about 3-5 minutes. Add the cranberries, sage, and mushrooms and cook, stirring frequently, 2-3 minutes.
4. Stir in bread crumbs, parsley, bacon, and broth and mix well. Transfer to a bowl to cool.
5. Remove the skin from the turkey, in one piece, do not discard. Butterfly the turkey breast and place between 2 sheets of plastic wrap. Pound out to ¼-inch thick.
6. Spread the stuffing over the turkey, leaving a ¾-inch border. Start with a short end and roll up the turkey. Wrap the skin back around the roll.
7. Use butcher string to tie the turkey. Place in the cooking pot and rub with butter. Sprinkle with salt.
8. Add the tender-crisp lid and set to roast on 400°F. Cook 20 minutes, then decrease the heat to 325°F. Cook another 10-15 minutes or until juices run clear. Let rest 10 minutes before slicing and serving.

Nutrition:

- InfoCalories 159,Total Fat 7g,Total Carbs 3g,Protein 19g,Sodium 120mg.

Chicken In Thai Peanut Sauce

Servings: 8
Cooking Time: 10 Minutes

Ingredients:

- 2 tbsp. oil
- 2 lbs. chicken thighs, boneless & skinless
- ½ cup chicken broth, low sodium
- ¼ cup soy sauce, low sodium
- 3 tbsp. cilantro, chopped
- 2 tbsp. lime juice
- ¼ tsp red pepper flakes
- 1 tsp ginger
- ¼ cup peanut butter
- 1 tbsp. corn starch
- 2 tbsp. water
- ¼ cup peanuts, chopped
- 2 green onions, sliced

Directions:

1. Add the oil to the cooking pot and set to sauté on med-high heat.
2. Add the chicken, in batches, and cook to brown all sides. Transfer to a plate.
3. Add the broth, soy sauce, cilantro, lime juice, pepper flakes, and ginger to the pot, stir to scrape up any brown bits on the bottom of the pot.
4. Stir in the peanut butter until melted. Return the chicken back to the pot and stir to coat with sauce.
5. Add the lid and set to pressure cook on high. Set the timer for 10 minutes. Once the timer goes off, use quick release to remove the pressure. Transfer chicken back to a plate.
6. In a small bowl, whisk together cornstarch and water until smooth. Stir mixture into the sauce and set the cooker back to sauté on medium heat.
7. Bring sauce to a boil, stirring constantly, and cook until sauce thickens, about 2-3 minutes. Add chicken and stir to coat wall. Serve garnished with peanuts and green onions.

Nutrition:

- InfoCalories 679,Total Fat 40g,Total Carbs 8g,Protein 72g,Sodium 2421mg.

Thyme Chicken With Veggies

Servings: 4

Cooking Time: 40 Min

Ingredients:

- 4 skin-on, bone-in chicken legs
- ½ cup dry white wine /125ml
- 1¼ cups chicken stock /312.5ml
- 1 cup carrots, thinly sliced /130g
- 1 cup parsnip, thinly sliced /130g
- 4 slices lemon
- 4 cloves garlic; minced
- 3 tomatoes, thinly sliced
- 2 tbsp olive oil /30ml
- 1 tbsp honey /15ml
- 1 tsp fresh chopped thyme /5g
- salt and freshly ground black pepper to taste
- Fresh thyme; chopped for garnish

Directions:

1. Season the chicken with pepper and salt. Warm oil on Sear/Sauté. Arrange chicken legs into the hot oil; cook for 3 to 5 minutes each side until browned. Place in a bowl and set aside. Cook thyme and garlic in the chicken fat for 1 minute until soft and lightly golden.

2. Add wine into the pot to deglaze, scrape the pot's bottom to get rid of any brown bits of food. Simmer the wine for 2 to 3 minutes until slightly reduced in volume.

3. Add stock, carrots, parsnips, tomatoes, pepper and salt into the pot.

4. Lay reversible rack onto veggies. Into the Foodi's steamer basket, arrange chicken legs. Set the steamer basket onto the reversible rack. Drizzle the chicken with honey then top with lemon slices.

5. Seal the pressure lid, choose Pressure, set to High, and set the timer to 12 minutes. Press Start. Release pressure naturally for 10 minutes. Place the chicken onto a bowl. Drain the veggies and place them around the chicken. Garnish with fresh thyme leaves before serving.

Korean Barbecued Satay

Servings: 4

Cooking Time: 4h 15 Min

Ingredients:

- 1 lb. boneless; skinless chicken tenders /450g
- ½ cup pineapple juice /125ml
- ½ cup soy sauce /125ml
- ⅓ cup sesame oil /84ml
- 4 scallions; chopped
- 1 pinch black pepper
- 4 cloves garlic; chopped
- 2 tsp sesame seeds, toasted /10g
- 1 tsp fresh ginger, grated /5g

Directions:

1. Skew each tender and trim any excess fat. Mix the other ingredients in one large bowl. Add the skewered chicken and place in the fridge for 4 to 24 hours.

2. Preheat the Foodi to 370 For 188°C. Using a paper towel, pat the chicken dry. Fry for 10 minutes on Air Crisp mode.

Healthy Chicken Stew

Servings: 4
Cooking Time: 4 Hours

Ingredients:

- 1 large potato, peeled & chopped
- 2 carrots, peeled & sliced
- ½ tsp salt
- ¼ tsp pepper
- 2 cloves garlic, chopped fine
- 3 cups chicken broth, low sodium
- 2 bay leaves
- 2 chicken breasts, boneless, skinless & cut in pieces
- ½ tsp thyme
- ¼ tsp basil
- 1 tsp paprika
- 2 tbsp. cornstarch
- ½ cup water
- 1 cup green peas

Directions:

1. Add the potatoes, carrots, salt, pepper, garlic, broth, bay leaves, chicken, thyme, basil, and paprika to the cooking pot, stir to mix.
2. Add the lid and set to slow cook on high. Cook 4 hours or until vegetables and chicken are tender.
3. In a small bowl, whisk together cornstarch and water until smooth. Stir into the cooking pot along with the peas.
4. Recover and cook another 15 minutes. Stir well before serving.

Nutrition:

- InfoCalories 187,Total Fat 2g,Total Carbs 25g,Protein 17g,Sodium 1038mg.

Herb Roasted Drumsticks

Servings: 3
Cooking Time: 40 Minutes

Ingredients:

- Nonstick cooking spray
- 1 tsp paprika
- ¼ tsp salt
- ½ tsp garlic powder
- ¼ tsp onion powder
- ¼ tsp dried thyme
- ¼ tsp pepper
- 6 chicken drumsticks, skin removed, rinsed & patted dry
- ½ tbsp. butter, melted

Directions:

1. Place the rack in the cooking pot and spray it with cooking spray.
2. In a small bowl, combine spices, mix well.
3. Place chicken on the rack and sprinkle evenly over chicken. Drizzle with melted butter.
4. Add the tender-crisp lid and set to roast on 375°F. Bake 35-40 minutes until juices run clear. Serve.

Nutrition:

- InfoCalories 319,Total Fat 12g,Total Carbs 0g,Protein 50g,Sodium 505mg.

Chicken With Mushroom Sauce

Servings: 10

Cooking Time: 6 Hours

Ingredients:

- 8 oz. tomato sauce
- 1 cup mushrooms, sliced
- ½ cup dry white wine
- 1 onion, chopped
- 1 clove garlic, chopped fine
- ¼ tsp salt
- ¼ tsp pepper
- 3 lbs. chicken pieces, skinless
- 2 tbsp. water
- 1 tbsp. flour

Directions:

1. Add the tomato sauce, mushrooms, wine, onion, garlic, salt and pepper to the cooking pot, stir to mix.
2. Add the chicken and turn to coat well
3. Add the lid and set to slow cook on low heat. Cook 6 hours or until chicken is cooked through and tender. Transfer chicken to a serving plate.
4. In a small bowl, whisk together water and flour until smooth. Stir into the sauce and cook 10-15 minutes, stirring frequently, until sauce thickens. Serve chicken topped with sauce.

Nutrition:

- InfoCalories 176,Total Fat 4g,Total Carbs 4g,Protein 28g,Sodium 164mg.

Turkey Breakfast Sausage

Servings: 8

Cooking Time: 10 Minutes

Ingredients:

- Nonstick cooking spray
- 1 lb. ground turkey
- ½ tsp sage
- ½ tsp marjoram
- ¾ tsp thyme
- ¼ tsp cayenne pepper
- ¼ tsp allspice
- ¼ tsp black pepper
- ¾ tsp salt
- 1 clove garlic, chopped fine
- ¼ cup maple syrup

Directions:

1. Spray the fryer basket with cooking spray and place in the cooking pot.
2. In a large bowl, mix all ingredients until combined. Form into 8 patties.
3. Place the sausage patties in the fryer basket in a single layer. Add the tender-crisp lid and set to air fry on 375°F. Cook about 10 minutes until browned on the outside and cooked through, turning over halfway through cooking time. Serve.

Nutrition:

- InfoCalories 126,Total Fat 7g,Total Carbs 7g,Protein 11g,Sodium 252mg.

Garlic-herb Chicken And Rice

Servings:4
Cooking Time: 14 Minutes
Ingredients:

- 1 box rice pilaf
- 1¾ cups water
- 1 tablespoon unsalted butter
- 4 boneless, skin-on chicken thighs
- 1 tablespoon extra-virgin olive oil
- 1 teaspoon kosher salt
- 1 teaspoon garlic powder

Directions:

1. Place the rice pilaf, water, and butter in the pot and stir.
2. Place Reversible Rack in pot, making sure it is in the higher position. Place the chicken thighs on the rack. Assemble pressure lid, making sure the pressure release valve is in the SEAL position.
3. Select PRESSURE and set to HI. Set time to 4 minutes. Select START/STOP to begin.
4. Stir together the olive oil, salt, and garlic powder in a small bowl.
5. When pressure cooking is complete, quick release the pressure by moving the pressure release valve to the VENT position. Carefully remove lid when unit has finished releasing pressure.
6. Brush the chicken with the olive oil mixture. Close crisping lid.
7. Select BROIL and set time to 10 minutes. Select START/STOP to begin.
8. When cooking is complete, serve the chicken with the rice.

Nutrition:

- InfoCalories: 451,Total Fat: 32g,Sodium: 577mg,Carbohydrates: 18g,Protein: 23g.

Asian Chicken

Servings: 4
Cooking Time: 35 Min
Ingredients:

- 1 lb. chicken; cut in stripes /450g
- 1 large onion
- 3 green peppers; cut in stripes
- 2 tomatoes; cubed
- 1 pinch fresh and chopped coriander
- 1 pinch ginger
- 1 tbsp mustard /15g
- 1 tbsp cumin powder /15g
- 2 tbsp oil /30ml
- Salt and black pepper

Directions:

1. Heat the oil in a deep pan. Add in the mustard, onion, ginger, cumin and green chili peppers. Sauté the mixture for 2-3 minutes. Then, add the tomatoes, coriander, and salt and keep stirring.
2. Coat the chicken with oil, salt, and pepper and cook for 25 minutes on Air Crisp mode at 380 °F or 194°C. Remove from the Foodi and pour the sauce over and around.

Chicken Tenders With Broccoli

Servings: 2

Cooking Time: 70 Min

Ingredients:

- 4 boneless; skinless chicken tenders
- 1 head broccoli; cut into florets
- ¼ cup barbecue sauce /62.5ml
- ¼ cup lemon marmalade /32.5g
- 1 cup basmati rice /130g
- 1 cup + 2 tbsp water/280ml
- ½ tbsp soy sauce /7.5ml
- 1 tbsp sesame seeds, for garnish /15g
- 2 tbsp sliced green onions, for garnish /30g
- 2 tbsp melted butter; divided /30ml
- ¼ tsp salt /1.25g
- ¼ tsp freshly ground black pepper /1.25g
- Cooking spray

Directions:

1. Pour the rice and water in the pot and stir to combine. Seal the pressure lid, choose Pressure, set to High, and the timer to 2 minutes. Press Start/Stop to boil the rice.

2. Meanwhile, in a medium bowl, toss the broccoli with 1 tbsp of melted butter, and season with the salt and black pepper. When done cooking, perform a quick pressure release, and carefully open the lid.

3. Place the reversible rack in the higher position inside the pot, which will be over the rice. Then, spray the rack with cooking spray. Lay the chicken tenders on the rack and brush with the remaining 1 tbsp of melted butter. Arrange the broccoli around the chicken tenders.

4. Close the crisping lid. Choose Air Crisp, set the temperature to 400°F, and set the time to 10 minutes. Press Start/Stop to begin. In a bowl, mix the barbecue sauce, lemon marmalade, and soy sauce until well combined. When done crisping, coat the chicken with the lemon sauce.

5. Use tongs to turn the chicken over and apply the lemon sauce in the other side. Close the crisping lid, select Broil and set the time to 5 minutes; press Start/Stop.

6. After cooking is complete, check for your desired crispiness and remove the rack from the pot. Spoon the rice into serving plates with the chicken and broccoli. Garnish with the sesame seeds and green onions and serve.

Italian Turkey & Pasta Soup

Servings: 8
Cooking Time: 10 Minutes
Ingredients:

- 1 lb. ground turkey sausage
- 1 onion, chopped fine
- 5 cloves garlic, chopped fine
- 1 green bell pepper, chopped fine
- 1 tbsp. Italian seasoning
- 2 15 oz. cans tomatoes, diced
- 2 8 oz. cans tomato sauce
- 4 cups chicken broth, low sodium
- 3 cups whole wheat pasta
- ¼ cup parmesan cheese
- ¼ cup mozzarella cheese, grated

Directions:

1. Add the sausage, onions, and garlic to the cooking pot. Set to sauté on med-high and cook, breaking sausage up, until meat is no longer pink and onions are translucent. Drain off excess fat.
2. Stir in bell pepper, Italian seasoning, tomatoes, tomato sauce, broth, and pasta, mix well.
3. Add the lid and set to pressure cook on high. Set the timer for 5 minutes. Once the timer goes off, use the natural release for 5-10 minutes, then quick release to remove the pressure.
4. Stir the soup and ladle into bowls. Serve garnished with parmesan and mozzarella cheeses.

Nutrition:

- InfoCalories 294,Total Fat 8g,Total Carbs 37g,Protein 22g,Sodium 841mg.

Chicken With Rice And Peas

Servings: 4
Cooking Time: 30 Min
Ingredients:

- 4 boneless; skinless chicken breasts; sliced
- 1 onion; chopped
- 1 celery stalk; diced
- 1 garlic clove; minced
- 2 cups chicken broth; divided /500ml
- 1 cup long grain rice /130g
- 1 cup frozen green peas /130g
- 1 tbsp oil olive /15ml
- 1 tbsp tomato puree /15ml
- ½ tsp paprika /2.5g
- ¼ tsp dried oregano/1.25g
- ¼ tsp dried thyme /1.25g
- ⅛ tsp cayenne pepper /0.625g
- ⅛ tsp ground white pepper /0.625g
- Salt to taste

Directions:

1. Season chicken with garlic powder, oregano, white pepper, thyme, paprika, cayenne pepper, and salt. Warm the oil on Sear/Sauté. Add in onion and cook for 4 minutes until fragrant. Mix in tomato puree to coat.
2. Add ¼ cup or 65ml chicken stock into the Foodi to deglaze the pan, scrape the pan's bottom to get rid of browned bits of food. Mix in celery, rice, and the seasoned chicken. Add in the remaining broth to the chicken mixture.
3. Seal the pressure lid, choose Pressure, set to High, and set the timer to 8 minutes. Press Start. Once ready, do a quick release. Mix in green peas, cover with the lid and let sit for 5 minutes. Serve warm.

Italian Chicken Muffins

Servings: 4

Cooking Time: 25 Minutes

Ingredients:

- Nonstick cooking spray
- 4 chicken breast halves, boneless & skinless
- ½ tsp salt, divided
- ½ tsp pepper, divided
- 1/3 cup part-skim ricotta cheese
- ¼ cup mozzarella cheese, grated
- 2 tbsp. parmesan cheese
- ½ tsp Italian seasoning
- ½ tsp garlic powder
- 2 tbsp. whole-wheat panko bread crumbs
- 1 tbsp. light butter, melted
- Paprika for sprinkling

Directions:

1. Place the rack in the cooking pot. Spray 4 cups of a 6- cup muffin tin.
2. Lay chicken between 2 sheets of plastic wrap and pound to ¼-inch thick. Season with ¼ teaspoon of salt and pepper.
3. In a medium bowl, combine ricotta, mozzarella, parmesan, Italian seasoning, garlic powder, and remaining salt and pepper, mix well. Spoon evenly onto centers of chicken. Wrap chicken around filling and place, seam side down, in prepared muffin cups.
4. In a small bowl, stir together bread crumbs and butter, sprinkle over the chicken then top with paprika.
5. Place muffin tin on rack and add the tender-crisp lid. Set to bake on 350°F. Cook chicken 25-30 minutes or until chicken is cooked through. Serve immediately.

Nutrition:

- InfoCalories 224,Total Fat 8g,Total Carbs 4g,Protein 31g,Sodium 485mg.

Smoked Turkey & Collard Greens

Servings: 6

Cooking Time: 35 Minutes

Ingredients:

- 1 smoked turkey leg, cooked
- 1 cup onion, chopped
- 3 cloves garlic, chopped fine
- 1 ½ cups chicken broth, low sodium
- 1 lb. fresh collard greens
- ¼ tsp red pepper flakes
- 1 tbsp. apple cider vinegar

Directions:

1. Add the turkey leg, onion, garlic, red pepper flakes, and broth to the cooking pot, stir to mix.
2. Add the collard greens to the pot and mix.
3. Add the lid and set to pressure cook on high. Set timer for 35 minutes. Once the timer goes off, use the quick release to remove the pressure.
4. Transfer turkey leg to a cutting board and use a fork to shred the meat. Return the meat to the pot. Stir in the vinegar and serve immediately.

Nutrition:

- InfoCalories 145,Total Fat 6g,Total Carbs 11g,Protein 16g,Sodium 786mg.

Sticky Drumsticks

Servings: 4

Cooking Time: 50 Min

Ingredients:

- 1 lb. drumsticks /450g
- 2 tbsp honey /30ml
- 2 tsp dijon mustard /10g
- Cooking spray
- Salt and pepper to taste

Directions:

1. Combine the honey, mustard, salt, and pepper in a large bowl. Add in the chicken and toss to coat. Cover and put in the fridge for 30 minutes.

2. Preheat your Foodi to 380 °F or 194°C. Grease the Foodi basket with cooking spray. Arrange the drumsticks on the basket. Cook for 20 minutes on Air Crisp mode. After 10 minutes, shake the drumsticks.

Chicken Meatballs Primavera

Servings: 4

Cooking Time: 30 Min

Ingredients:

- 1 lb. ground chicken /450g
- ½ lb. chopped asparagus /225g
- 1 cup chopped tomatoes /130g
- 1 cup chicken broth /250ml
- 1 red bell pepper, seeded and sliced
- 2 cups chopped green beans /260g
- 1 egg, cracked into a bowl
- 2 tbsp chopped basil + extra to garnish /30g
- 1 tbsp olive oil + ½ tbsp olive oil /22.5ml
- 6 tsp flour /30g
- 1 ½ tsp Italian Seasoning /7.5g
- Salt and black pepper to taste

Directions:

1. In a mixing bowl, add the chicken, egg, flour, salt, pepper, 2 tbsps of basil, 1 tbsp of olive oil, and Italian seasoning. Mix them well with hands and make 16 large balls out of the mixture. Set the meatballs aside.

2. Select Sear/Sauté mode. Heat half tsp of olive oil, and add peppers, green beans, and asparagus. Cook for 3 minutes, stirring frequently.

3. After 3 minutes, use a spoon the veggies onto a plate and set aside. Pour the remaining oil in the pot to heat and then fry the meatballs in it in batches. Fry them for 2 minutes on each side to brown them lightly.

4. After, put all the meatballs back into the pot as well as the vegetables. Also, pour the chicken broth over it.

5. Close the lid, secure the pressure valve, and select Pressure mode on High pressure for 10 minutes. Press Start/Stop. Do a quick pressure release. Close the crisping lid and select Air Crisp. Cook for 5 minutes at 400 °F or 205°C, until nice and crispy.

6. Dish the meatballs with sauce into a serving bowl and garnish it with basil. Serve with over cooked pasta.

Crunchy Chicken Schnitzels

Servings: 4

Cooking Time: 25 Min

Ingredients:

- 4 chicken breasts, boneless
- 2 eggs, beaten
- 4 slices cold butter
- 4 slices lemon
- 1 cup flour /130g
- 1 cup breadcrumbs /130g
- 2 tbsp fresh parsley; chopped 30g
- Cooking spray
- Salt and pepper to taste

Directions:

1. Combine the breadcrumbs with the parsley in a dish and set aside. Season the chicken with salt and pepper. Coat in flour; shake off any excess. Dip the coated chicken into the beaten egg followed by breadcrumbs. Spray the schnitzels with cooking spray.

2. Put them into the Foodi basket, close the crisping lid and cook for 10 minutes at 380 °F or 194°C. After 5 minutes, turn the schnitzels over. Arrange the schnitzels on a serving platter and place the butter and lemon slices over to serve.

Shredded Chicken & Black Beans

Servings: 4

Cooking Time: 4 Hours

Ingredients:

- 16 oz. fresh salsa
- 15 oz. black beans, rinsed & drained
- 1 lb. chicken thighs, boneless & skinless
- 1/3 cup cheddar cheese, reduced fat, grated
- 1 tsp cumin
- ½ tsp chili powder
- 1/8 tsp salt
- 1/8 tsp pepper

Directions:

1. Place the salsa, beans, and chicken in the cooking pot. Add the lid and set to slow cook on high. Cook 3 ½ hours or until chicken is tender.

2. Transfer chicken to a cutting board and use 2 forks to shred. Return to the pot.

3. Stir in remaining ingredients and mix well. Cook another 15 minutes or until cheese is melted. Serve immediately.

Nutrition:

- InfoCalories 283,Total Fat 6g,Total Carbs 25g,Protein 33g,Sodium 1474mg.

Chicken Thighs With Cabbage

Servings: 4

Cooking Time: 35 Min

Ingredients:

- 1 pound green cabbage, shredded /450g
- 4 slices pancetta; diced
- 4 chicken thighs, boneless skinless
- 1 cup chicken broth /250ml
- 1 tbsp Dijon mustard/15g
- 1 tbsp lard /15g
- Fresh parsley; chopped
- salt and ground black pepper to taste

Directions:

1. Warm lard on Sear/Sauté. Fry pancetta for 5 minutes until crisp. Set aside. Season chicken with pepper and salt. Sear in Foodi for 2 minutes each side until browned. In a bowl, mix mustard and chicken broth.

2. In your Foodi, add pancetta and chicken broth mixture. Seal the pressure lid, choose Pressure, set to High, and set the timer to 6 minutes. Press Start. When ready, release the pressure quickly.

3. Open the lid, mix in green cabbage, seal again, and cook on High Pressure for 2 minutes. When ready, release the pressure quickly. Serve with sprinkled parsley.

Rosemary Lemon Chicken

Servings: 2

Cooking Time: 60 Min

Ingredients:

- 2 chicken breasts
- 2 rosemary sprigs
- ½ lemon; cut into wedges
- 1 tbsp oyster sauce /15ml
- 3 tbsp brown sugar /45g
- 1 tbsp soy sauce /15ml
- ½ tbsp olive oil /7.5ml
- 1 tsp minced ginger /5g

Directions:

1. Place the ginger, soy sauce, and olive oil, in a bowl. Add the chicken and coat well. Cover the bowl and refrigerate for 30 minutes. Transfer the marinated chicken to the Foodi basket.

2. Close the crisping lid and cook for about 6 minutes on Air Crisp mode at 370 F. or 188°C

3. Mix the oyster sauce, rosemary and brown sugar in a small bowl. Pour the sauce over the chicken. Arrange the lemon wedges in the dish. Return to the Foodi and cook for 13 more minutes on Air Crisp mode.

Chicken Cassoulet With Frijoles

Servings: 4

Cooking Time: 60 Min

Ingredients:

- 4 small chicken thighs, bone-in skin-on
- 2 pancetta slices; cut into thirds
- 1 medium carrot; diced
- ½ small onion; diced
- Olive oil, as needed
- ½ cup dry red wine /125ml
- 1 cup Pinto Beans Frijoles; soaked /130g
- 3 cups chicken stock /750ml
- 1 cup panko breadcrumbs /130g
- 1½ tsp salt /7.5g
- ¼ tsp black pepper /1.25g

Directions:

1. Season the chicken on both sides with salt and black pepper and set aside on a wire rack. On your Foodi, choose Sear/Sauté and adjust to Medium. Press Start to preheat the inner pot.

2. Add the pancetta slices in a single layer and cook for 3 to 4 minutes or until browned on one side. Turn and brown the other side. Remove the pancetta to a paper towel-lined plate.

3. Put the chicken thighs in the pot, and fry for about 6-7 minutes or until is golden brown on both sides. Use tongs to pick the chicken into a plate.

4. Carefully pour out all the fat in the pot leaving about 1 tbsp to coat the bottom of the pot. Reserve the remaining fat in a small bowl.

5. Sauté the carrots and onion in the pot for 3 minutes with frequent stirring, until the onion begins to brown. Stir in the wine while scraping off the brown bits at the bottom. Allow boiling until the wine reduces by one-third and stir in the beans and chicken stock.

6. Seal the pressure lid, choose pressure; adjust the pressure to High and the cook time to 25 minutes. Press Start to commence cooking.

7. When done cooking, perform a quick pressure release and carefully open the lid. Return the chicken to the pot and cook for 10 minutes.

8. Combine the breadcrumbs with the reserved fat until evenly mixed. When done cooking, perform a natural pressure release for 5 minutes, then a quick pressure release to let out any remaining steam, and carefully open the lid.

9. Crumble the pancetta over the cassoulet. Spoon the breadcrumbs mixture on top of the beans while avoiding the chicken as much as possible.

10. Close the crisping lid; choose Broil, adjust the cook time to 7 minutes, and press Start/Stop. When the cassoulet is ready, allow resting for a few minutes before serving.

Chapter 4 Beef, Pork & Lamb

Beef Sirloin Steak

Servings: 4

Cooking Time: 17 Minutes

Ingredients:

- 3 tablespoons butter
- 1/2 teaspoon garlic powder
- 1-2 pounds beef sirloin steaks
- Black pepper and salt to taste
- 1 garlic clove, minced

Directions:

1. Select "Sauté" mode on your Ninja Foodi and add butter; let the butter melt.
2. Stir in beef sirloin steaks.
3. Sauté for 2 minutes on each side.
4. Add garlic powder, garlic clove, salt, and pepper.
5. Lock and secure the Ninja Foodi's lid and cook on "Medium-High" pressure for 15 minutes.
6. Release pressure naturally over 10 minutes.
7. Transfer prepare Steaks to a serving platter, enjoy.

Nutrition:

- InfoCalories: 246; Fat: 13g; Carbohydrates: 2g; Protein: 31g

Stuffed Cabbage Rolls

Servings: 6

Cooking Time: 5 Hours

Ingredients:

- 12 cabbage leaves
- 3 ¼ tsp salt, divided
- 15 oz. tomato sauce
- 2 tbsp. honey
- 1 tsp paprika
- ½ tsp thyme
- 2 tbsp. lemon juice
- 2 tbsp. ketchup
- 1 tsp Worcestershire sauce
- 1 ¼ tsp pepper
- 1 cup long grain brown rice, cooked
- 1 egg, beaten
- ¼ cup milk
- ¼ cup onion, chopped fine
- 1 clove garlic, chopped fine
- 1 lb. lean ground beef

Directions:

1. Fill a large pot with water and add 2 teaspoons salt. Bring to a boil on high heat. Add cabbage leaves and boil 2 minutes. Transfer leaves to a plate and let cool.
2. In a medium bowl, whisk together tomato sauce, honey, spices, lemon juice, ketchup, Worcestershire, remaining salt, and pepper until smooth.
3. In a separate bowl, combine rice, egg, milk, onion, garlic, and beef. Stir in ¼ of the sauce and mix well.
4. Spoon ¼ cup of beef mixture into the center of each cabbage leaf. Roll up, tucking in the ends. Place in the cooking pot. Pour remaining sauce over the rolls.
5. Add the lid and set to slow cook in high. Cook 4-5 hours until cabbage is tender and filling is cooked through. Serve.

Nutrition:

- InfoCalories 282,Total Fat 10g,Total Carbs 25g,Protein 24g,Sodium 1732mg.

Beef Stew With Veggies

Servings: 6

Cooking Time: 1 Hr 15 Min

Ingredients:

- 2 pounds beef chuck; cubed /900g
- 1 cup dry red wine /250ml
- 3 cups carrots; chopped /390g
- ¼ cup flour /32.5g
- 2 cups beef stock /500ml
- 4 cups potatoes; diced /520g
- 1 onion; diced
- 3 garlic cloves; minced
- 2 celery stalks; chopped
- 3 tomatoes; chopped
- 2 bell pepper, thinly sliced
- 1 tbsp dried Italian seasoning /15g
- 2 tbsp olive oil /30ml
- 2 tbsp butter /30g
- 2 tsp salt; divided /10g
- 1 tsp paprika /5g
- 1 tsp ground black pepper/5g
- 2 tsp Worcestershire sauce /10ml
- A handful of fresh parsley; chopped
- salt and ground black pepper to taste

Directions:

1. In a bowl, mix black pepper, beef, flour, paprika, and 1 tsp salt. Toss the ingredients and ensure the beef is coated. Warm butter and oil on Sear/Sautét. Add in beef and cook for 8- 10 minutes until browned. Set aside on a plate.

2. To the same fat, add garlic, onion, and celery, bell peppers, and cook for 4-5 minutes until tender.

3. Deglaze with wine, scrape the bottom to get rid of any browned beef bits. Pour in remaining salt, beef stock, Worcestershire sauce, and Italian seasoning. Return beef to the pot; add carrots, tomatoes, and potatoes.

4. Seal the pressure lid, choose Pressure, set to High, and set the timer to 35 minutes. Press Start. Release pressure naturally for 10 minutes. Taste and adjust the seasonings as necessary. Serve on plates and scatter over the parsley.

Bacon-wrapped Hot Dogs

Servings:4
Cooking Time: 15 Minutes
Ingredients:

- 4 beef hot dogs
- 4 bacon strips
- Cooking spray

- 4 bakery hot dog buns, split and toasted
- ½ red onion, chopped
- 1 cup sauerkraut, rinsed and drained

Directions:

1. Place Cook & Crisp Basket in pot. Close crisping lid. Select AIR CRISP, set temperature to 360°F, and set time to 5 minutes. Select START/STOP to begin preheating.
2. Wrap each hot dog with 1 strip of bacon, securing it with toothpicks as needed.
3. Once unit has preheated, open lid and coat the basket with cooking spray. Place the hot dogs in the basket in a single layer. Close crisping lid.
4. Select AIR CRISP, set temperature to 360°F, and set time to 15 minutes. Select START/STOP to begin.
5. After 10 minutes, open lid and check doneness. If needed, continue cooking until it reaches your desired doneness.
6. When cooking is complete, place the hot dog in the buns with the onion and sauerkraut. Top, if desired, with condiments of your choice, such as yellow mustard, ketchup, or mayonnaise.

Nutrition:

- InfoCalories: 336,Total Fat: 17g,Sodium: 1297mg,Carbohydrates: 27g,Protein: 20g.

Swedish Meatballs With Mashed Cauliflower

Servings: 6
Cooking Time: 1 Hr
Ingredients:

- ¾ pound ground pork /337.5g
- ¾ pound ground beef /337.5g
- 1 head cauliflower; cut into florets
- 1 large egg, beaten
- ½ onion; minced
- 1 ¾ cup heavy cream; divided /438ml
- ¼ cup bread crumbs /32.5g
- ¼ cup sour cream /62.5ml

- 2 cups beef stock /500ml
- ¼ cup fresh chopped parsley /32.5g
- 1 tbsp water /15ml
- 4 tbsp butter; divided /60g
- 3 tbsp flour /45g
- ½ tsp red wine vinegar /2.5ml
- salt and freshly ground black pepper to taste

Directions:

1. In a mixing bowl, mix ground beef, onion, salt, bread crumbs, ground pork, egg, water, and pepper; shape meatballs. Warm 2 tbsp or 30g of butter on Sear/Sauté.
2. Add meatballs and cook until browned, about 5-6 minutes. Set aside to a plate. Pour beef stock in the pot to deglaze, scrape the pan to get rid of browned bits of food.
3. Stir vinegar and flour with the liquid in the pot until smooth; bring to a boil. Stir ¾ cup heavy cream into the liquid. Arrange meatballs into the gravy. Place trivet onto meatballs. Arrange cauliflower florets onto the trivet.
4. Seal the pressure lid, choose Pressure, set to High, and set the timer to 8 minutes. Press Start.When ready, release the pressure quickly.
5. Set the cauliflower in a mixing bowl. Add in the remaining 1 cup or 250ml heavy cream, pepper, sour cream, salt, and 2 or 30g tbsp butter and use a potato masher to mash the mixture until smooth.
6. Spoon the mashed cauliflower onto serving bowls; place a topping of gravy and meatballs. Add parsley for garnishing.

Cuban Flank Steak

Servings: 6
Cooking Time: 8 Hours
Ingredients:

- 15 oz. tomatoes, crushed
- 1 tbsp. apple cider vinegar
- 2 cloves garlic, chopped fine
- 1 tbsp. cumin
- 1 jalapeño, chopped fine
- 2 lbs. flank steak
- 2 red bell peppers, chopped
- 1 onion, chopped
- ½ tsp salt
- ¼ cup black olives, pitted & chopped
- 3 tbsp. green onions, sliced

Directions:

1. Add all ingredients, except the olives, to the cooking pot. Stir to coat.
2. Add the lid and set to slow cook on low. Cook 8 hours or until beef is tender.
3. Transfer beef to a large bowl and shred, using 2 forks. Return the beef to the pot.
4. Add the olives and stir to combine. Serve as is garnished with green onions, or over hot, cooked rice.

Nutrition:

- InfoCalories 348,Total Fat 13g,Total Carbs 11g,Protein 45g,Sodium 380mg.

Beef Brisket & Carrots

Servings: 10
Cooking Time: 8 Hours 15 Minutes
Ingredients:

- 4 -5 lb. beef brisket,
- 1 ½ tsp salt
- 3 onions, sliced
- 6 cloves garlic, chopped fine
- 1 sprig thyme
- 1 sprig rosemary
- 4 bay leaves
- 2 cups beef broth, low sodium
- 3 carrots, peeled & sliced ½-inch thick
- 1 tbsp. mustard

Directions:

1. Use a sharp knife and score the fat side of the brisket in parallel lines, being careful to only slice through the fat, not the meat. Repeat to create a cross-hatch pattern. Sprinkle with salt and let sit 30 minutes.

2. Set the cooker to sear on med-high and lay brisket, fat side down, in the pot. Cook 5-8 minutes to render the fat. Turn the brisket over and brown the other side. Transfer to a plate.

3. Add the onions and season with salt. Cook, stirring frequently, until onions are browned, about 5-8 minutes. Add the garlic and cook 1 minute more.

4. Stir in remaining ingredients. Add the brisket back to the pot, pushing it down to cover as much as possible by the broth.

5. Add the lid and set to slow cook on low. Cook 8-9 hours or until brisket is tender. Transfer brisket to cutting board and tent with foil. Let rest 10-15 minutes. Slice across the grain to serve with carrots, onions and some of the cooking liquid.

Nutrition:

- InfoCalories 143,Total Fat 10g,Total Carbs 2g,Protein 10g,Sodium 833mg.

Beef Mole

Servings: 8

Cooking Time: 8 Hours

Ingredients:

- 2 lbs. beef stew meat, cut in 1-inch cubes
- 3 tsp salt, divided
- 2 tbsp. olive oil
- 2 onions, chopped fine
- 4 cloves garlic, chopped fine
- 1 chili, seeded & chopped fine
- 3 tsp chili powder
- 1 tsp ancho chili powder
- 2 tsp oregano
- 2 tsp cumin
- 1 tsp paprika
- 1 lb. dried red beans, soaked in water overnight, drained
- 5 cups water
- 2 cups beer
- 2 15 oz. tomatoes, crushed
- 1 tbsp. brown sugar
- 2 oz. unsweetened chocolate, chopped
- 1 bay leaf
- 3 tbsp. lime juice

Directions:

1. Place the beef in a large Ziploc bag with 1 ½ teaspoons salt, seal and rub gently to massage the salt into the meat. Refrigerate overnight.
2. Add the oil to the cooking pot and set to sauté on med-high heat.
3. Working in batches, add the beef and cook until deep brown on all sides. Transfer to a bowl.
4. Add the onions to the pot and cook about 5 minutes or until softened. Stir in garlic, chilies, remaining salt, chili powders, oregano, cumin, and paprika and cook 1 minute more.
5. Stir in beans, water, beer, tomatoes, brown sugar, and chocolate and mix well. Stir in the beef and add the bay leaf.
6. Add the lid and set to slow cook on low. Cook 8 hours or until beef is tender. Stir in lime juice and serve.

Nutrition:

- InfoCalories 127,Total Fat 8g,Total Carbs 7g,Protein 7g,Sodium 310mg.

Beef And Cherry Tagine

Servings: 4

Cooking Time: 1 Hr 20 Min

Ingredients:

- 1 ½ pounds stewing beef, trimmed /675g
- 1 onion; chopped
- 1-star anise
- ¼ cup toasted almonds, slivered /32.5g
- 1 cup dried cherries, halved /130g
- 1 cup water /250ml
- 1 tbsp honey /15ml
- 2 tbsp olive oil /30ml
- ¼ tsp ground allspice /1.25g
- 1 tsp ground cinnamon /5g
- ½ tsp paprika /2.5g
- ½ tsp turmeric /2.5g
- ½ tsp salt /2.5g
- ¼ tsp ground ginger /1.25g

Directions:

1. Set your Foodi to Sear/Sauté, set to Medium High, and choose Start/Stop to preheat the pot. Warm olive oil. Add in onions and cook for 3 minutes until fragrant. Mix in beef and cook for 2 minutes each side until browned.
2. Stir in anise, cinnamon, turmeric, allspice, salt, paprika, and ginger; cook for 2 minutes until aromatic.
3. Add in honey and water. Seal the pressure lid, choose Pressure, set to High, and set the timer to 50 minutes. Press Start.
4. Meanwhile, in a bowl, soak dried cherries in hot water until softened. Once ready, release pressure naturally for 15 minutes. Drain cherries and stir into the tagine. Top with toasted almonds before serving.

Beef Bourguignon(1)

Servings: 4

Cooking Time: 30 Minutes

Ingredients:

- 1-pound stewing steak
- 1/2-pound bacon
- 5 medium carrots, diced
- 1 large red onion, peeled and sliced
- 2 garlic cloves, minced
- 2 teaspoons salt
- 2 tablespoons fresh thyme
- 2 tablespoons fresh parsley, chopped
- 2 teaspoons ground pepper
- 1/2 cup beef broth
- 1 tablespoon olive oil
- 1 tablespoon sugar-free maple syrup

Directions:

1. Select "Sauté" mode on your Ninja Foodi and stir in 1 tablespoon of oil, allow the oil to heat up.
2. Pat your beef dry and season it well.
3. Stir in beef into the Ninja Foodi in batches and Sauté them until nicely browned up.
4. Slice up the cooked bacon into strips and add the strips to the pot.
5. Add onions as well and brown them.
6. Stir in the rest of the listed ingredients and lock up the lid.
7. Cook for 30 minutes on "HIGH" pressure.
8. Allow the pressure to release naturally over 10 minutes. Enjoy.

Nutrition:

- InfoCalories: 416; Fats: 18g; Carbohydrates: 12g; Protein:27g

Lime Glazed Pork Tenderloin

Servings: 8
Cooking Time: 45 Minutes
Ingredients:

- ¼ cup honey
- 1/3 cup lime juice
- 1 tsp lime zest, grated
- 2 cloves garlic, chopped fine
- 2 tbsp. yellow mustard
- ½ tsp salt
- ½ tsp pepper
- 2 pork tenderloins, 1 lb. each, fat trimmed
- Nonstick cooking spray

Directions:

1. In a large Ziploc bag combine, honey, lime juice, zest, garlic, mustard, salt, and pepper. Seal the bag and shake to mix.
2. Add the tenderloins and turn to coat. Refrigerate overnight.
3. Spray the rack with cooking spray and add it to the cooking pot.
4. Place the tenderloins on the rack, discard marinade. Add the tender-crisp lid and set to roast on 400°F. Cook tenderloins 40-45 minutes or until they reach desired doneness. Transfer to serving plate and let rest 10 minutes before slicing and serving.

Nutrition:

- InfoCalories 162,Total Fat 3g,Total Carbs 10g,Protein 24g,Sodium 249mg.

Beef And Bacon Chili

Servings: 6
Cooking Time: 1 Hr
Ingredients:

- 2 pounds stewing beef, trimmed /900g
- 29 ounces canned whole tomatoes /870g
- 15 ounces canned kidney beans, drained and rinsed /450g
- 4 ounces smoked bacon; cut into strips /120g
- 1 chipotle in adobo sauce, finely chopped
- 1 onion; diced
- 2 bell peppers; diced
- 3 garlic cloves; minced
- 2 cups beef broth /500ml
- 1 tbsp ground cumin/15g
- 2 tsp olive oil; divided /10ml
- 1 tsp chili powder /5g
- ½ tsp cayenne pepper /2.5g
- 4 tsp salt; divided /20g
- 1 tsp freshly ground black pepper; divided /5g

Directions:

1. Set on Sear/Sauté, set to Medium High, and choose Start/Stop to preheat the pot and fry the bacon until crispy, about 5 minutes. Set aside.
2. Rub the beef with ½ tsp or 5g black pepper and 1 tsp or 5g salt. In the bacon fat, brown beef for 5-6 minutes; transfer to a plate.
3. Warm the oil. Add in garlic, peppers and onion and cook for 3 to 4 minutes until soft. Stir in cumin, cayenne pepper, the extra pepper and salt; chopped chipotle, and chili powder and cook for 30 seconds until soft.
4. Return beef and bacon to the pot with vegetables and spices; add in tomatoes and broth.
5. Seal the pressure lid, choose Pressure, set to High, and set the timer to 45 minutes. Press Start. When ready, release the pressure quickly. Stir in beans. Let simmer on Keep Warm for 10 minutes until flavors combine.

Cheddar Cheeseburgers

Servings: 4
Cooking Time: 20 Min
Ingredients:

- 1 lb. ground beef /900g
- 1 packet dry onion soup mix /30g
- 4 burger buns
- 4 tomato slices
- 4 Cheddar cheese slices
- 4 small leaves lettuce
- 1 cup water /250ml
- Mayonnaise
- Ketchup
- Mustard

Directions:

1. In a bowl, add beef and onion mix, and mix well with hands. Shape in 4 patties and wrap each in foil paper. Pour the water into the inner steel insert of Foodi, and fit in the steamer rack. Place the wrapped patties on the trivet, close the lid, and secure the pressure valve, and cook on 10 minutes on Pressure mode on High pressure.
2. Once the timer has stopped, do a natural pressure release for 5 minutes, then a quick pressure release to let out the remaining steam.
3. Use a set of tongs to remove the wrapped beef onto a flat surface and carefully unwrap the patties.
4. To assemble the burgers:
5. In each half of the buns, put a lettuce leaf, then a beef patty, a slice of cheese, and a slice of tomato. Top it with the other halves of buns. Serve with some ketchup, mayonnaise, and mustard.

Bacon Strips

Servings: 2
Cooking Time: 7 Minutes
Ingredients:

- 10 bacon strips
- 1/4 teaspoon chilli flakes
- 1/3 teaspoon salt
- 1/4 teaspoon basil, dried

Directions:

1. Rub the bacon strips with chilli flakes, dried basil, and salt.
2. Turn on your air fryer and place the bacon on the rack.
3. Lower the air fryer lid. Cook the bacon at 400 °F for 5 minutes.
4. Cook for 3 minutes more if the bacon is not fully cooked. Serve and enjoy.

Nutrition:

- InfoCalories: 500; Fat: 46g; Carbohydrates: 0g; Protein: 21g

Mississippi Pot Roast With Potatoes

Servings: 6
Cooking Time: 1 Hr 40 Min
Ingredients:

- 2 pounds chuck roast /900g
- 5 potatoes, peeled and sliced
- 10 pepperoncini
- 2 bay leaves
- 1 onion, finely chopped
- ½ cup pepperoncini juice /125ml
- 6 cups beef broth /1500ml
- ¼ cup butter /32.5g
- 1 tbsp canola oil /15ml
- ½ tsp dried thyme /2.5g
- ½ tsp dried parsley /2.5g
- 1 tsp onion powder /5g
- 1 tsp garlic powder /5g
- 2 tsp salt /10g
- ½ tsp black pepper /2.5g

Directions:

1. Warm oil on Sear/Sauté. Season chuck roast with pepper and salt, then sear in the hot oil for 2 to 4 minutes for each side until browned. Set aside.
2. Melt butter and cook onion for 3 minutes until fragrant. Sprinkle with dried parsley, onion powder, dried thyme, and garlic powder and stir for 30 seconds.
3. Into the pot, stir bay leaves, beef broth, pepperoncini juice, and pepperoncini. Nestle chuck roast down into the liquid. Seal the pressure lid, choose Pressure, set to High, and set the timer to 60 minutes. Press Start.
4. Release pressure naturally for about 10 minutes. Set the chuck roast to a cutting board and use two forks to shred. Serve immediately.

Beef Stir Fry

Servings: 4
Cooking Time: 11 Minutes
Ingredients:

- 1 lb. beef sirloin, sliced into strips
- 1 tablespoon vegetable oil
- 1-1/2 lb. broccoli florets
- 1 red bell pepper, sliced into strips
- 1 yellow pepper, sliced into strips
- 1 green bell pepper, sliced into strips
- 1/2 cup onion, sliced into strips
- Marinade:
- 1/4 cup of hoisin sauce
- 1 teaspoon sesame oil
- 2 teaspoons garlic, minced
- 1 teaspoon of ground ginger
- 1 tablespoon soy sauce
- 1/4 cup of water

Directions:

1. Put all the marinade ingredients in a suitable. Divide it in half.
2. Soak the beef in the marinade for 20 minutes. Toss the vegetables in the other half.
3. Place the vegetables in the Ninja Foodi basket. Seal the crisping lid.
4. Select air crisp. Cook at 200 °F for 5 minutes.
5. Remove the vegetables and set them aside. Put the meat on the basket.
6. Seal and cook at 360 °For 6 minutes.

Nutrition:

- InfoCalories: 390; Fat: 13g; Carbohydrate: 28.9g; Protein: 41.3g

Honey Short Ribs With Rosemary Potatoes

Servings: 4

Cooking Time: 105 Min

Ingredients:

- 4 bone-in beef short ribs, silver skin
- 2 potatoes, peeled and cut into 1-inch pieces
- ½ cup beef broth /125ml
- 3 garlic cloves; minced
- 1 onion; chopped
- 2 tbsp olive oil /30ml
- 2 tbsp honey /30ml
- 2 tbsp minced fresh rosemary /30ml
- 1 tsp salt /5g
- 1 tsp black pepper /5g

Directions:

1. Choose Sear/Sauté on the pot and set to High. Choose Start/Stop to preheat the pot. Season the short ribs on all sides with ½ tsp or 2.5g of salt and ½ tsp or 2.5g of pepper. Heat 1 tbsp of olive oil and brown the ribs on all sides, about 10 minutes total. Stir in the onion, honey, broth, 1 tbsp of rosemary, and garlic.

2. Seal the pressure lid, choose Pressure, set to High, and set the time to 40 minutes. Choose Start/Stop to begin. In a large bowl, toss the potatoes with the remaining oil, rosemary, salt, and black pepper.

3. When the ribs are ready, perform a quick pressure release and carefully open the lid.

4. Fix the reversible rack in the higher position of the pot, which is over the ribs. Put the potatoes on the rack. Close the crisping lid. Choose Bake/Roast, set the temperature to 350°F or 177°C, and set the time to 15 minutes. Choose Start/Stop to begin roasting.

5. Once the potatoes are tender and roasted, use tongs to pick the potatoes and the short ribs into a plate; set aside. Choose Sear/Sauté and set to High. Simmer the sauce for 5 minutes and spoon the sauce into a bowl.

6. Allow sitting for 2 minutes and scoop off the fat that forms on top. Serve the ribs with the potatoes and sauce.

Carne Guisada

Servings: 4

Cooking Time: 45 Minutes

Ingredients:

- 3 pounds beef stew
- 3 tablespoon seasoned salt
- 1 tablespoon oregano chilli powder
- 1 tablespoon cumin
- 1 pinch crushed red pepper
- 2 tablespoons olive oil
- 1/2 medium lime, juiced
- 1 cup beef bone broth
- 3 ounces tomato paste
- 1 large onion, sliced

Directions:

1. Trim the beef stew to taste into small bite-sized portions.
2. Toss the beef stew pieces with dry seasoning.
3. Select "Sauté" mode on your Ninja Foodi and stir in oil; allow the oil to heat up.
4. Add seasoned beef pieces and brown them.
5. Combine the browned beef pieces with the rest of the ingredients.
6. Lock the Ninja foodi's lid and cook on "HIGH" pressure for 3 minutes.
7. Release the pressure naturally.
8. Enjoy.

Nutrition:

- InfoProtein: 33g; Carbohydrates: 11g; Fats: 12g; Calories: 274

Beef Pho With Swiss Chard

Servings: 6

Cooking Time: 1 Hr 10 Min

Ingredients:

- 2 pounds Beef Neck Bones /900g
- 10 ounces sirloin steak /300g
- 8 ounces rice noodles /240g
- 1 yellow onion, quartered
- A handful of fresh cilantro; chopped
- 2 scallions; chopped
- 2 jalapeño peppers; sliced
- ¼ cup minced fresh ginger /32.5g
- 9 cups water /2250ml
- 2 cups Swiss chard; chopped /260g
- 2 tsp coriander seeds /10g
- 2 tsp ground cinnamon /10g
- 2 tsp ground cloves /10g
- 2 tbsp coconut oil /30ml
- 3 tbsp sugar /45g
- 2 tbsp fish sauce /30ml
- 2 ½ tsp kosher salt /12.5g
- Freshly ground black pepper to taste

Directions:

1. Melt the oil on Sear/Sauté. Add ginger and onions and cook for 4 minutes until the onions are softened. Stir in cloves, cinnamon and coriander seeds and cook for 1 minute until soft. Add in water, salt, beef meat and bones.

2. Seal the pressure lid, choose Pressure, set to High, and set the timer to 30 minutes. Press Start. Release pressure naturally for 10 minutes.

3. Transfer the meat to a large bowl; cover with it enough water and soak for 10 minutes. Drain the water and slice the beef. In hot water, soak rice noodles for 8 minutes until softened and pliable; drain and rinse with cold water. Drain liquid from cooker into a separate pot through a fine-mesh strainer; get rid of any solids.

4. Add fish sauce and sugar to the broth; transfer into the Foodi and simmer on Sear/Sauté. Place the noodles in four separate soup bowls. Top with steak slices, scallions, swiss chard; sliced jalapeño pepper, cilantro, red onion, and pepper. Spoon the broth over each bowl to serve.

Italian Pasta Potpie

Servings:8
Cooking Time: 55 Minutes

Ingredients:

- 5 cups, plus 1 teaspoon water, divided
- 1 box rigatoni pasta
- 4 fresh Italian sausage links
- 1 bag frozen cooked meatballs
- 16 ounces whole milk ricotta
- 1 jar marinara sauce
- 2 cups shredded mozzarella cheese
- 1 refrigerated store-bought pie crust, room temperature
- 1 large egg

Directions:

1. Pour 5 cups of water and the rigatoni in the pot. Assemble pressure lid, making sure the pressure release valve is in the SEAL position.
2. Select PRESSURE and set to LO. Set time to 0 minutes. Select START/STOP to begin.
3. When pressure cooking is complete, quick release the pressure by turning the pressure release valve to the VENT position. Carefully remove lid when unit has finished releasing pressure.
4. Drain the pasta and set it aside, keeping warm. Wipe out pot and return it to base. Insert Cook & Crisp Basket into pot. Close crisping lid.
5. Select AIR CRISP, set temperature to 390°F, and set time to 15 minutes. Select START/STOP to begin. Let preheat for 5 minutes.
6. Open lid and place the sausages in the basket. Close lid and cook for 10 minutes.
7. When cooking is complete, remove sausages to a cutting board. Add the meatballs to the basket. Close crisping lid.
8. Select AIR CRISP, set temperature to 390°F, and set time to 10 minutes. Select START/STOP to begin.
9. Slice sausages into very thin rounds.
10. When cooking is complete, transfer the meatballs to the cutting board and slice them in half.
11. In the pot, in this order, add a layer of ricotta, marinara sauce, sausage, mozzarella cheese, pasta, marinara sauce, meatballs, mozzarella cheese, pasta, ricotta, and marinara sauce. Place the pie crust on top of the filling.
12. In a small bowl, whisk together the egg and remaining 1 teaspoon of water. Brush this on top of the pie crust. With a knife, slice a couple of small holes in the middle of crust to vent it. Close crisping lid.
13. Select BAKE/ROAST, set temperature to 350°F, and set time to 30 minutes. Select START/STOP to begin.
14. When cooking is complete, open lid. Let sit for 10 minutes before serving.

Nutrition:

- InfoCalories: 821,Total Fat: 41g,Sodium: 1414mg,Carbohydrates: 67g,Protein: 40g.

Beef, Barley & Mushroom Stew

Servings: 8

Cooking Time: 1 Hour 15 Minutes

Ingredients:

- 2 tbsp. butter, unsalted
- 2 lbs. beef chuck, cubed
- 1 tsp salt
- 3 cups onions, chopped
- 1 lb. mushrooms, sliced
- 1 quart beef broth, low sodium
- 3 cups water
- 2 tsp marjoram
- 1 cup pearl barley
- 1 cup carrot, chopped
- 3 cups turnips, peeled & chopped
- ½ tsp pepper
- ½ cup sour cream
- 8 small sprigs fresh dill

Directions:

1. Add the butter to the cooking pot and set to sauté on medium heat.
2. Working in batches, cook the beef until brown on all sides, seasoning with salt as it cooks. Transfer browned beef to a bowl.
3. Add the onions and cook, stirring up brown bits from the bottom of the pot, about 5-6 minutes or until they begin to brown.
4. Add the mushrooms and increase heat to med-high. Cook 2-3 minutes.
5. Add the beef back to the pot and stir in marjoram, broth, and water, stir to mix.
6. Add the lid and set to pressure cook on high. Set timer for 30 minutes. When timer goes off use quick release to remove the pressure.
7. Stir in barley, turnips, and carrots. Add the lid and pressure cook on high another 30 minutes. When the timer goes off, use quick release to remove the pressure.
8. Ladle into bowls and garnish sour cream and dill. Serve immediately.

Nutrition:

- InfoCalories 67,Total Fat 2g,Total Carbs 5g,Protein 7g,Sodium 162mg.

Polynesian Pork Burger

Servings: 4
Cooking Time: 25 Minutes
Ingredients:

- 1 lb. ground pork
- ¼ cup green onion, chopped fine
- 1/8 tsp allspice
- 1/8 tsp salt
- 1/8 tsp pepper
- ½ tsp ginger
- 4 pineapple rings
- ¼ cup barbecue sauce
- 4 burger buns
- 4 large lettuce leaves
- ¼ lb. ham, sliced thin

Directions:

1. Spray the rack with cooking spray and place it in the cooking pot.
2. In a large bowl, combine pork, green onion, allspice, salt, pepper, and ginger until thoroughly mixed. Form into 4 patties.
3. Place the patties on the rack and brush the tops with barbecue sauce. Add the tender-crisp lid and set to broil. Cook patties 5-7 minutes, flip and brush with barbecue sauce, cook another 5-7 minutes. Place the patties on the bottom of the cooking pot.
4. Spray the rack with cooking spray again. Lay the pineapple rings on the rack. Cook 3-5 minutes per side. Transfer pineapple and patties to a serving plate and let sit 5 minutes.
5. Place the buns on the rack, cut side up, and toast. To serve; top bottom bun with lettuce, then patty, barbecue sauce, ham, pineapple and top bun. Repeat. Serve immediately.

Nutrition:

- InfoCalories 155,Total Fat 7g,Total Carbs 13g,Protein 10g,Sodium 279mg.

Chinese Bbq Ribs

Servings: 6
Cooking Time: 8 Hours
Ingredients:

- 4 tbsp. hoisin sauce
- 4 tbsp. oyster sauce
- 2 tbsp. soy sauce, low sodium
- 2 tbsp. rice wine
- 2 lbs. pork ribs, cut in 6 pieces
- Nonstick cooking spray
- 2-inch piece fresh ginger, grated
- 3 green onions, sliced
- 2 tbsp. honey

Directions:

1. In a large bowl, whisk together hoisin sauce, oyster sauce, soy sauce, and rice wine. Add the ribs and turn to coat. Cover and refrigerate overnight.
2. Spray the cooking pot with cooking spray.
3. Add the ribs and marinade. Top with ginger and green onions. Add the lid and set to slow cook on low. Cook 6-8 hours or until ribs are tender.
4. Transfer ribs to a serving plate. Spray the rack with the cooking spray and place in the pot. Lay the ribs, in a single layer, on the rack and brush with honey.
5. Add the tender-crisp lid and set to broil. Cook 3-4 minutes to caramelize the ribs. Serve.

Nutrition:

- InfoCalories 135,Total Fat 4g,Total Carbs 6g,Protein 17g,Sodium 419mg.

Pork Chops With Squash Purée And Mushroom Gravy

Servings: 4
Cooking Time: 45 Min
Ingredients:

- 4 pork chops
- 1 pound butternut squash; cubed /450g
- 2 sprigs rosemary, leaves removed and chopped
- 2 sprigs thyme, leaves removed and chopped
- 4 cloves garlic; minced
- 1 cup mushrooms; chopped /130g

- 1 cup chicken broth /250ml
- 1 tbsp olive oil /15ml
- 2 tbsp olive oil /30ml
- 1 tbsp soy sauce /15ml
- 1 tsp cornstarch 5g

Directions:

1. Set on Sear/Sauté, set to Medium High, and choose Start/Stop to preheat the pot and heat rosemary, thyme and 1 tbsp or 15ml of olive oil. Add the pork chops and sear for 1 minute for each side until lightly browned.

2. Sauté garlic and mushrooms in the pressure cooker for 5-6 minutes until mushrooms are tender. Add soy sauce and chicken broth. Transfer pork chops to a wire trivet and place it into the pressure cooker. Over the chops, place a cake pan. Add butternut squash in the pot and drizzle with 1 tbsp olive oil.

3. Seal the pressure lid, choose Pressure, set to High, and set the timer to 10 minutes. Press Start. When ready, release the pressure quickly. Remove the pan and trivet from the pot. Stir cornstarch into the mushroom mixture for 2 to 3 minutes until the sauce thickens.

4. Transfer the mushroom sauce to an immersion blender and blend until you attain the desired consistency. Scoop sauce into a cup with a pour spout. Smash the squash into a purée. Set pork chops on a plate and ladle squash puree next to them. Top the pork chops with gravy.

Beef And Bell Pepper With Onion Sauce

Servings: 6
Cooking Time: 62 Min
Ingredients:

- 2 lb. round steak pieces, about 6 to 8 pieces /900g
- ½ yellow bell pepper, finely chopped
- 1 yellow onion, finely chopped
- 2 cloves garlic; minced
- ½ green bell pepper, finely chopped

- ½ red bell pepper, finely chopped
- ¼ cup flour /32.5g
- ½ cup water /125ml
- 2 tbsp olive oil /30ml
- Salt and pepper, to taste

Directions:

1. Wrap the steaks in plastic wrap, place on a cutting board, and use a rolling pin to pound flat of about 2-inch thickness. Remove the plastic wrap and season them with salt and pepper. Set aside.

2. Put the chopped peppers, onion, and garlic in a bowl, and mix them evenly. Spoon the bell pepper mixture onto the flattened steaks and roll them to have the peppers inside.

3. Use some toothpicks to secure the beef rolls and dredge the steaks in all-purpose flour while shaking off any excess flour. Place them in a plate.

4. Select Sear/Sauté mode on Foodi and heat the oil. Add the beef rolls and brown them on both sides, for about 6 minutes.

5. Pour the water over the meat, close the lid, secure the pressure valve, and select Pressure mode on High pressure for 20 minutes. Press Start/Stop.

6. Once the timer has stopped, do a natural pressure release for 10 minutes. Close the crisping lid and cook for 10 minutes on Broil mode. When ready, Remove the meat to a plate and spoon the sauce from the pot over. Serve the stuffed meat rolls with a side of steamed veggies.

Barbeque Sticky Baby Back Ribs With

Servings: 6
Cooking Time: 40 Min
Ingredients:

- 1 reversible rack baby back ribs; cut into bones
- 1/3 cup ketchup /88ml
- 1 cup barbecue sauce /250ml
- ½ cup apple cider /125ml
- 1 tbsp mustard powder /15g

- 1 tbsp smoked paprika /15g
- 2 tbsp olive oil /30ml
- 1 tbsp dried oregano/15g
- ½ tsp ground black pepper /2.5g
- ½ tsp salt /2.5g

Directions:
1. In a bowl, thoroughly combine salt, mustard powder, smoked paprika, oregano, and black pepper. Rub the mixture over the ribs. Warm oil on Sear/Sauté.
2. Add in the ribs and sear for 1 to 2 minutes for each side until browned. Pour apple cider and barbecue sauce into the pot. Turn the ribs to coat.
3. Seal the pressure lid, choose Pressure, set to High, and set the timer to 30 minutes. Press Start. When ready, release the pressure quickly.
4. Place the Cook & Crisp Basket in the pot. Close the crisping lid, choose Air Crisp, set the temperature to 390°F or 199°C, and the time to 5 minutes.
5. Place the ribs with the sauce in the Cook & Crisp Basket. Close the Crisping Lid. Preheat the unit by selecting Air Crisp, setting the temperature to 390°F or 199°C, and setting the time to 7 minutes. Press Start. When ready, the ribs should be sticky with a brown dark color. Transfer the ribs to a serving plate. Baste with the sauce to serve.

Italian Pot Roast

Servings: 8
Cooking Time: 8 Hours
Ingredients:

- 1 tsp salt
- ½ tsp pepper
- 1 tsp garlic powder
- 1 tsp onion powder
- 2 tsp Italian seasoning
- 6 oz. tomato paste

- 2 lb. beef sirloin roast
- 1 onion, sliced thin
- 1 green bell pepper, sliced thin
- 1 banana pepper, sliced thin
- ½ cup beef broth, low sodium

Directions:
1. In a small bowl, combine salt, pepper, garlic powder, onion powder, Italian seasoning, and tomato paste, mix well.
2. Coat the roast, on all sides, with spice mixture and place in the cooking pot. Place the onions and peppers on top of the roast and pour in the broth.
3. Add the lid and set to slow cook on low. Cook 7-8 hours or until beef is tender.
4. You can slice the beef and serve topped with the onions and peppers. Or, you can shred the beef and use it to make sandwiches.

Nutrition:
- InfoCalories 270,Total Fat 16g,Total Carbs 6g,Protein 24g,Sodium 392mg.

Short Ribs With Egg Noodles

Servings: 4

Cooking Time: 65 Min

Ingredients:

- 4 pounds bone-in short ribs /1800g
- 1 garlic clove; minced
- 1½ cups panko bread crumbs /195g
- Low-sodium beef broth
- 6 ounces egg noodles /180g
- 3 tbsp melted unsalted butter /45ml
- 2 tbsp prepared horseradish /30g
- 6 tbsp Dijon mustard /90g
- 2½ tsp salt /12.5g
- ½ tsp freshly ground black pepper /2.5g

Directions:

1. Season the short ribs on all sides with 1½ tsp s or 7.5g of salt. Pour 1 cup 250ml of broth into the inner pot. Put the reversible rack in the lower position in the pot, and place the short ribs on top. Seal the pressure lid, choose Pressure; adjust the pressure to High and the time to 25 minutes; press Start. After cooking, perform a natural pressure release for 5 minutes, then a quick pressure release, and carefully open the lid. Remove the rack and short ribs.

2. Pour the cooking liquid into a measuring cup to get 2 cups. If lesser than 2 cups, add more broth and season with salt and pepper.

3. Add the egg noodles and the remaining salt. Stir and submerge the noodles as much as possible. Seal the pressure lid, choose Pressure; adjust the pressure to High and the cook time to 4 minutes; press Start.

4. In a bowl, combine the horseradish, Dijon mustard, garlic, and black pepper. Brush the sauce on all sides of the short ribs and reserve any extra sauce.

5. In a bowl, mix the butter and breadcrumbs. Coat the ribs with the crumbs. Put the ribs back on the rack. After cooking, do a quick pressure release, and carefully open the lid. Stir the noodles, which may not be quite done but will continue cooking.

6. Return the rack and beef to the pot in the upper position.

7. Close the crisping lid and Choose Bake/Roast; adjust the temperature to 400°F or 205°C and the cook time to 15 minutes. Press Start. After 8 minutes, open the lid and turn the ribs over. Close the lid and continue cooking. Serve the beef and noodles, with the extra sauce on the side, if desired.

Orecchiette And Pork Ragu

Servings:6

Cooking Time: 25 Minutes

Ingredients:

- 3 tablespoons extra-virgin olive oil, divided
- 1 pound pork shoulder, cut into large pieces
- 1 small onion, diced
- 1 carrot, diced
- 1 celery stalk, diced
- 1 garlic clove, minced
- 1 can crushed tomatoes
- 1 can tomato purée
- 1 cup red wine
- 2 cups beef stock
- 1 box orecchiette pasta
- 1 teaspoon sea salt
- 1 teaspoon Italian seasoning
- 1 bunch Tuscan kale, ribs and stems removed, torn
- ¼ cup unsalted butter, cubed
- ½ cup grated Parmesan cheese

Directions:

1. Select SEAR/SAUTÉ and set to HI. Select START/STOP to begin. Let preheat for 5 minutes.

2. Place 2 tablespoons of oil in the pot. Once hot, add the pork pieces and sear on all sides, turning until brown, about 10 minutes in total. Transfer the pork to a large plate and set aside.

3. Add onion, carrot, and celery and cook for about 5 minutes. Add the garlic and cook for 1 minute.

4. Add the crushed tomatoes, tomato purée, red wine, beef stock, pasta, salt, and Italian seasoning. Place the pork back in the pot. Assemble pressure lid, making sure the pressure release valve is in the SEAL position.

5. Select PRESSURE and set to LO. Set time to 0 minutes. Select START/STOP to begin.

6. When pressure cooking is complete, allow pressure to naturally release for 10 minutes. After 10 minutes, quick release remaining pressure by moving the pressure release valve to the VENT position. Carefully remove lid when unit has finished releasing pressure.

7. Pull the pork pieces apart using two forks. Add the remaining 1 tablespoon of olive oil, kale, butter, and Parmesan cheese and stir until the butter melts and the kale is wilted. Serve.

Nutrition:

- InfoCalories: 556,Total Fat: 21g,Sodium: 1277mg,Carbohydrates: 59g,Protein: 30g.

Cheesy Taco Pasta Bake

Servings:6

Cooking Time: 20 Minutes

Ingredients:

- 1 tablespoon extra-virgin olive oil
- 1 small onion, diced
- 1 pound ground beef
- 1 packet taco seasoning
- 1 can diced tomatoes
- 1 can diced green chiles
- 1 box dry elbow pasta
- 4 cups beef broth
- 2 ounces cream cheese, cut into pieces
- 3 cups shredded Mexican blend cheese, divided
- Optional toppings:
- Sour cream, for garnish
- Red onion, for garnish
- Chopped cilantro, for garnish

Directions:

1. Select SEAR/SAUTÉ and set to MD:HI. Select START/STOP to begin. Let preheat for 5 minutes.

2. Place the oil, onion, and beef in the pot and cook for about 5 minutes, using a wooden spoon to break apart the beef as it cooks. Add the taco seasoning and mix until the beef is coated.

3. Add the tomatoes, green chiles, pasta, and beef broth. Assemble pressure lid, making sure the pressure release valve is in the SEAL position.

4. Select PRESSURE and set to LO. Set time to 0 minutes. Select START/STOP to begin.

5. When pressure cooking is complete, allow pressure to naturally release for 10 minutes. After 10 minutes, quick release remaining pressure by moving the pressure release valve to the VENT position. Carefully remove lid when unit has finished releasing pressure.

6. Add the cream cheese and 2 cups of cheese. Stir well to melt cheese and ensure all ingredients are combined. Cover the pasta evenly with the remaining 1 cup of cheese. Close crisping lid.

7. Select BROIL and set time to 5 minutes. Select START/STOP to begin.

8. When cooking is complete, serve immediately.

Nutrition:

- InfoCalories: 633,Total Fat: 40g,Sodium: 1154mg,Carbohydrates: 36g,Protein: 37g.

Chapter 5 Fish & Seafood

Indian Cod & Basmati Rice

Servings: 8

Cooking Time: 30 Minutes

Ingredients:

- 1 ½ tsp turmeric, divided
- 2 tsp chili powder
- 1 ¼ tsp salt, divided
- 2 lbs. cod, cut in large pieces
- 3 tbsp. butter
- 1 onion, chopped
- 1 tsp ginger, grated
- 4 bay leaves
- 1 cinnamon stick
- 5 whole cloves
- 5 cardamom pods
- 1 tsp ground coriander
- 1 tsp garam masala
- 2 cups water
- 1 cup coconut milk, unsweetened
- 3 Roma tomatoes, seeded & chopped
- 4 tbsp. cilantro, chopped, divided
- 1 tbsp. fresh mint, chopped
- 3 cups brown basmati rice, rinsed & drained

Directions:

1. In a small bowl, combine ½ teaspoon turmeric, chili powder, and ¼ teaspoon salt. Sprinkle over fish and let sit 20 minutes.

2. Add the butter to the cooking pot and set to sauté on medium heat. Add onion and cook until soft.

3. Add ginger along with all the remaining spices and cook 1-2 minutes until fragrant.

4. Add the fish and cook, stirring gently, until cooked through, about 2-3 minutes. Transfer fish to a plate and turn off the sauté mode.

5. Add the water and coconut milk, and stir, scraping up any brown bits from the bottom of the pot. Add tomatoes, 3 tablespoons cilantro, and mint, stir to mix.

6. Sprinkle the rice on top and stir gently to make sure it is covered with liquid. Add the lid and set to pressure cook on high. Set the timer for 20 minutes.

7. When the timer goes off, use natural release to remove the lid. All of the liquid should be absorbed, if not, cook another 5 minutes.

8. To serve, fluff the rice and discard whole spices, spoon onto plates, top with fish and chopped cilantro.

Nutrition:

- InfoCalories 465,Total Fat 14g,Total Carbs 60g,Protein 24g,Sodium 774mg.

Cheesy Crab Pie

Servings: 8
Cooking Time: 40 Minutes
Ingredients:

- 1 cup cheddar cheese, grated
- 1 pie crust, uncooked
- 1 cup crab meat
- 3 eggs
- 1 cup half and half, fat free
- ½ tsp salt
- ¼ tsp pepper
- ½ tsp lemon zest

Directions:

1. Place the rack in the cooking pot.
2. Spread the cheese in an even layer in the bottom of the pie crust. Top with crab.
3. In a medium bowl, whisk together remaining ingredients until combined. Pour over crab.
4. Place the pie on the rack and add the tender-crisp lid. Set to bake on 325°F. Bake 40 minutes until filling is set and the top is lightly browned. Let cool 10 minutes before serving.

Nutrition:

- InfoCalories 246,Total Fat 14g,Total Carbs 18g,Protein 11g,Sodium 469mg.

Parmesan Tilapia

Servings: 4
Cooking Time: 15 Min
Ingredients:

- ¾ cup grated Parmesan cheese /98g
- 4 tilapia fillets
- 1 tbsp olive oil /15ml
- 1 tbsp chopped parsley /15g
- ¼ tsp garlic powder /1.25g
- 2 tsp paprika /10g
- ¼ tsp salt /1.25g

Directions:

1. Mix parsley, Parmesan, garlic, salt, and paprika, in a shallow bowl. Brush the olive oil over the fillets, and then coat them with the Parmesan mixture.
2. Place the tilapia onto a lined baking sheet, and then into the Ninja Foodi.
3. Close the crisping lid and cook for about 4 to 5 minutes on all sides on Air Crisp mode at 350 °F or 177°C.

Fried Salmon

Servings: 1

Cooking Time: 13 Min

Ingredients:

- 1 salmon fillet.
- ¼ tsp garlic powder /1.25g
- 1 tbsp soy sauce /15ml
- Salt and pepper

Directions:

1. Combine the soy sauce with the garlic powder, salt, and pepper. Brush the mixture over the salmon. Place the salmon onto a sheet of parchment paper and inside the Ninja Foodi.

2. Close the crisping lid and cook for 10 minutes on Air Crisp at 350 °F or 177°C, until crispy on the outside and tender on the inside.

Crab Alfredo

Servings: 4

Cooking Time: 25 Minutes

Ingredients:

- ½ cup butter, unsalted
- ½ red bell pepper, seeded & chopped
- 2 tbsp. cream cheese, low fat
- 2 cups half and half
- ¾ cup parmesan cheese, reduced fat
- 1 tsp garlic powder
- 2 cups penne pasta, cooked & drained
- 6 oz. lump crab meat, cooked

Directions:

1. Add butter to the cooking pot and set to sauté on medium heat.
2. When butter has melted, add bell pepper and cook until it starts to soften, about 3-5 minutes.
3. Add the cream cheese and cook, stirring until it melts.
4. Stir in half and half and parmesan cheese, and garlic powder until smooth. Reduce heat to low and simmer 15 minutes.
5. Stir in cooked penne and crab meat and cook just until heated through. Serve immediately.

Nutrition:

- InfoCalories 388,Total Fat 23g,Total Carbs 26g,Protein 19g,Sodium 613mg.

Stir Fried Scallops & Veggies

Servings: 6
Cooking Time: 15 Minutes
Ingredients:

- 2 tbsp. peanut oil
- 3 cloves garlic, chopped fine
- 1 tsp crushed red pepper flakes
- 1 lb. bay scallops
- 2 tbsp. sesame seeds
- 1 ½ tsp ginger
- 1 head bok choy, trimmed and chopped
- 16 oz. stir-fry vegetables
- 1 tbsp. soy sauce, low sodium

Directions:

1. Add the oil to the cooking pot and set to saute on med-high heat.
2. Add the garlic, red pepper flakes, and scallops and cook until scallops are golden brown and cooked. Transfer scallops to a bowl and keep warm.
3. Add the sesame seeds and ginger and cook, stirring, 1-2 minutes until all the liquid is gone.
4. Add the cabbage and vegetables and cook 4-5 minutes, stirring occasionally.
5. Add the soy sauce and return the scallops to the pot. Cook 1-2 minutes more until heated through. Serve immediately.

Nutrition:

- InfoCalories 172,Total Fat 5g,Total Carbs 17g,Protein 15g,Sodium 485mg.

Lemon Cod Goujons And Rosemary Chips

Servings: 4
Cooking Time: 100 Min
Ingredients:

- 4 cod fillets, cut into strips
- 2 potatoes, cut into chips
- 4 lemon wedges to serve
- 2 eggs
- 1 cup arrowroot starch /130g
- 1 cup flour /130g
- 2 tbsps olive oil /30ml
- 3 tbsp fresh rosemary; chopped /45g
- 1 tbsp cumin powder /15g
- ½ tbsp cayenne powder /7.5g
- 1 tsp black pepper, plus more for seasoning /5g
- 1 tsp salt, plus more for seasoning /5g
- Zest and juice from 1 lemon
- Cooking spray

Directions:

1. Fix the Crisping Basket in the pot and close the crisping lid. Choose Air Crisp, set the temperature to 375°F or 191°C, and the time to 5 minutes. Choose Start/Stop to preheat the pot.
2. In a bowl, whisk the eggs, lemon zest, and lemon juice. In another bowl, combine the arrowroot starch, flour, cayenne powder, cumin, black pepper, and salt.
3. Coat each cod strip in the egg mixture, and then dredge in the flour mixture, coating well on all sides. Grease the preheated basket with cooking spray. Place the coated fish in the basket and oil with cooking spray.
4. Close the crisping lid. Choose Air Crisp, set the temperature to 375°F or 191°C, and the time to 15 minutes; press Start/Stop. Toss the potatoes with oil and season with salt and pepper.
5. After 15 minutes, check the fish making sure the pieces are as crispy as desired. Remove the fish from the basket.
6. Pour the potatoes in the basket. Close the crisping lid; choose Air Crisp, set the temperature to 400°F or 205°C, and the time to 24 minutes; press Start/Stop.
7. After 12 minutes, open the lid, remove the basket and shake the fries. Return the basket to the pot and close the lid to continue cooking until crispy.
8. When ready, sprinkle with fresh rosemary. Serve the fish with the potatoes and lemon wedges.

Curried Salmon & Sweet Potatoes

Servings: 4

Cooking Time: 20 Minutes

Ingredients:

- Nonstick cooking spray
- 2 sweet potatoes, peeled & cubed
- 1 tbsp. + 1 tsp olive oil, divided
- ½ tsp salt
- 1 tsp thyme
- 1 tsp curry powder
- 1 tsp honey
- ½ tsp lime zest
- 1/8 tsp crushed red pepper flakes
- 4 salmon filets

Directions:

1. Spray the cooking pot with cooking spray.
2. In a large bowl, combine potatoes, 1 tablespoon oil, salt, and thyme and toss to coat the potatoes. Place in the cooking pot.
3. Add the tender-crisp lid and set to roast on 400°F. Cook potatoes 10 minutes.
4. In a small bowl, whisk together remaining oil, curry powder, honey, zest, and pepper flakes. Lay the salmon on a sheet of foil and brush the curry mixture over the top.
5. Open the lid and stir the potatoes. Add the rack to the cooking pot and place the salmon, with the foil, on the rack. Close the lid and continue to cook another 10-15 minutes until potatoes are tender and fish flakes easily with a fork. Serve.

Nutrition:

- InfoCalories 239,Total Fat 8g,Total Carbs 15g,Protein 25g,Sodium 347mg.

Cod With Ginger And Scallion Sauce

Servings:4

Cooking Time: 10 Minutes

Ingredients:

- 2 tablespoons rice vinegar
- 2 tablespoons soy sauce
- 1 tablespoon chicken stock
- 1 tablespoon grated fresh ginger
- 4 skinless cod fillets
- Sea salt
- Freshly ground black pepper
- Greens of 6 scallions, thinly sliced

Directions:

1. In a small bowl, mix together the rice vinegar, soy sauce, chicken stock, and ginger.
2. Season the cod fillets on both sides with salt and pepper. Place them in the pot and cover with the vinegar mixture.
3. Select SEAR/SAUTÉ and set to MED. Bring the liquid to a low boil.
4. Once boiling, turn the heat to LO and cover with the pressure lid. Cook for 8 minutes.
5. Remove lid and add the scallion greens to the top of the fish. Cover with the pressure lid and cook for 2 minutes more. Serve.

Nutrition:

- InfoCalories: 149,Total Fat: 2g,Sodium: 642mg,Carbohydrates: 2g,Protein: 30g.

Salmon Chowder

Servings: 8
Cooking Time: 30 Minutes
Ingredients:

- 3 tbsp. butter
- ½ cup celery, chopped
- ½ cup onion, chopped
- ½ cup green bell pepper, chopped
- 1 clove garlic, chopped fine
- 14 ½ oz. chicken broth, low sodium
- 1 cup potatoes, peeled & cubed
- 1 cup carrots, chopped
- 1 tsp salt
- ½ tsp pepper
- 1 tsp fresh dill, chopped
- 1 can cream-style corn
- 2 cups half and half
- 2 cups salmon, cut in 1-inch pieces

Directions:

1. Add the butter to the cooking pot and set to sauté on med-high heat.
2. Add the celery, onion, green pepper, and garlic and cook, stirring frequently, until vegetables start to soften.
3. Add the broth, potatoes, carrots, salt, pepper and dill and stir to mix.
4. Add the lid and set to pressure cook on high. Set the timer for 10 minutes. When the timer goes off, release the pressure with quick release.
5. Set back to sauté on medium and add the corn, cream, and salmon. Bring to a simmer and cook 15 minutes, or until salmon is cooked through. Serve.

Nutrition:

- InfoCalories 244,Total Fat 10g,Total Carbs 21g,Protein 18g,Sodium 905mg.

Pistachio Crusted Salmon

Servings: 1
Cooking Time: 15 Min
Ingredients:

- 1 salmon fillet
- 3 tbsp pistachios /45g
- 1 tsp grated Parmesan cheese /5g
- 1 tsp lemon juice /5ml
- 1 tsp mustard /5g
- 1 tsp olive oil /5ml
- Pinch of sea salt
- Pinch of garlic powder
- Pinch of black pepper

Directions:

1. Whisk the mustard and lemon juice together. Season the salmon with salt, pepper, and garlic powder. Brush the olive oil on all sides.
2. Brush the mustard-lemon mixture on top of the salmon. Chop the pistachios finely, and combine them with the Parmesan cheese.
3. Sprinkle them on top of the salmon. Place the salmon in the Ninja Foodi basket with the skin side down.
4. Close the crisping lid and cook for 10 minutes on Air Crisp mode at 350 °F or 177°C.

Stuffed Cod

Servings: 4

Cooking Time: 40 Minutes

Ingredients:

- ½ cup bread crumbs
- 2 ½ tsp garlic powder, divided
- 1 ½ tsp onion powder, divided
- 1 tbsp. parsley
- ¼ cup parmesan cheese
- ½ tsp salt
- ½ lb. scallops, rinsed & dried
- 7 tbsp. butter, divided
- ½ lb. shrimp, peeled & deveined
- 1 tbsp. flour
- ¾ cup chicken broth, low sodium
- ½ tsp dill
- ½ cup sour cream
- ½ tbsp. lemon juice
- 4 cod filets, patted dry

Directions:

1. Set cooker to bake on 400°F. Place the rack in the cooking pot.
2. In a small bowl, combine bread crumbs, 2 teaspoons garlic powder, 1 teaspoon onion powder, parsley, parmesan cheese, and salt, mix well.
3. Place the scallops in a baking pan and pour 3 tablespoons melted butter over top. Add the bread crumb mixture, and with a spatula mix together so scallops are coated on all sides.
4. Cover with foil and place in the cooking pot. Add the tender-crisp lid and bake 10 minutes.
5. Uncover and add the shrimp and 3 tablespoons butter to the scallops, use the spatula again to coat the shrimp. Recover the dish and bake another 10 minutes. Remove from cooking pot and uncover to cool.
6. In a small saucepan over medium heat, melt the remaining tablespoon of butter. Add the flour and cook, whisking, for 1 minute.
7. Whisk in broth, remaining garlic and onion powder, and dill until combined. Bring mixture just to boil, whisking constantly, and cook until thickened, about 5 minutes. Remove from heat let cool 5 minutes before stirring in sour cream and lemon juice.
8. Pour the scallop mixture onto a cutting board and chop. Add it back to the baking dish.
9. Spoon stuffing mixture onto the wide end of the fish filets and fold in half. Secure with a toothpick. Place on a small baking sheet.
10. Spoon a small amount of the sauce over fish and place on the rack in the cooking pot. Set to bake on 375°F. Add the tender-crisp lid and cook 20 minutes. Transfer to serving plates and top with more sauce. Serve immediately.

Nutrition:

- InfoCalories 483,Total Fat 27g,Total Carbs 19g,Protein 41g,Sodium 1459mg.

Classic Crab Imperial

Servings: 6
Cooking Time: 20 Minutes
Ingredients:

- 1 cup mayonnaise
- 2 eggs, lightly beaten
- 2 tsp sugar
- 2 tsp Old Bay seasoning
- 1 tsp lemon juice
- 2 tsp parsley, chopped fine
- 2 lb. jumbo lump crab meat

Directions:

1. In a medium bowl, combine mayonnaise, eggs, sugar, Old Bay, lemon juice, and parsley and mix well.
2. Gently fold in crab. Divide evenly between 6 ramekins and place in the cooking pot.
3. Add the tender-crisp lid and set to bake on 350°F. Bake 20-25 minutes until the top is golden brown. Let cool slightly before serving.

Nutrition:

- InfoCalories 382,Total Fat 18g,Total Carbs 10g,Protein 43g,Sodium 1201mg.

Crab Cakes

Servings: 4
Cooking Time: 55 Min
Ingredients:

- ½ cup cooked crab meat /65g
- ¼ cup breadcrumbs /32.5g
- ¼ cup chopped celery /32.5g
- ¼ cup chopped red pepper /32.5g
- ¼ cup chopped red onion /32.5g
- Zest of ½ lemon
- 3 tbsp mayonnaise /45mk
- 1 tbsp chopped basil /15g
- 2 tbsp chopped parsley /30g
- Old Bay seasoning, as desired
- Cooking spray

Directions:

1. Place all Ingredients in a large bowl and mix well until thoroughly incorporated. Make 4 large crab cakes from the mixture and place on a lined sheet. Refrigerate for 30 minutes, to set.
2. Spay the air basket with cooking spray and arrange the crab cakes in it.
3. Close the crisping lid and cook for 7 minutes on each side on Air Crisp at 390 °F or 199°C.

Sweet & Spicy Shrimp Bowls

Servings: 8
Cooking Time: 5 Minutes
Ingredients:

- ½ cup green onions, chopped
- 1 jalapeno pepper, seeded & chopped
- 1 tsp red chili flakes
- 8 oz. crushed pineapple, drained
- 2 tbsp. honey
- 1 lime, zested & juiced
- 1 tbsp. olive oil
- 2 lbs. large shrimp, peeled & deveined
- ¼ tsp salt
- 2 cups brown rice, cooked

Directions:

1. In a small bowl, combine green onions, jalapeno, chili flakes, pineapple, honey, lime juice, and zest and mix well.
2. Add the oil to the cooking pot and set to saute on medium heat.
3. Sprinkle the shrimp with salt and cook, 3-5 minutes or until they turn pink.
4. Add the shrimp to the pineapple mixture and stir to coat.
5. Spoon rice into bowls and top with shrimp mixture. Serve immediately.

Nutrition:

- InfoCalories 188,Total Fat 3g,Total Carbs 23g,Protein 17g,Sodium 644mg.

Potato Chowder With Peppery Prawns

Servings: 4
Cooking Time: 80 Min
Ingredients:

- 4 slices serrano ham; chopped
- 16 ounces frozen corn /500g
- 16 prawns, peeled and deveined
- 1 onion; chopped
- 2 Yukon Gold potatoes; chopped
- ¾ cup heavy cream /188ml
- 2 cups vegetable broth /500ml
- 2 tbsps olive oil /30ml
- 4 tbsps minced garlic; divided /60g
- 1 tsp dried rosemary /5g
- 1 tsp salt; divided /5g
- 1 tsp freshly ground black pepper; divided /5g
- ½ tsp red chili flakes /2.5g

Directions:

1. Choose Sear/Sauté on the pot and set to Medium High. Choose Start/Stop to preheat the pot. Add 1 tbsp or 15ml of the olive oil and cook the serrano ham, 2 tbsps of garlic, and onion, stirring occasionally; for 5 minutes. Fetch out one-third of the serrano ham into a bowl for garnishing.
2. Add the potatoes, corn, vegetable broth, rosemary, half of the salt, and half of the black pepper to the pot.
3. Seal the pressure lid, hit Pressure and set to High. Set the time to 10 minutes, and press Start.
4. In a bowl, toss the prawns in the remaining garlic, salt, black pepper, the remaining olive oil, and the red chili flakes. When done cooking, do a quick pressure release and carefully open the pressure lid.
5. Stir in the heavy cream and fix the reversible rack in the pot over the chowder.
6. Spread the prawn in the rack. Close the crisping lid. Choose Broil and set the time to 8 minutes. Choose Start/Stop. When the timer has ended, remove the rack from the pot.
7. Ladle the corn chowder into serving bowls and top with the prawns. Garnish with the reserved ham and serve immediately.

Mussel Chowder With Oyster Crackers

Servings: 4
Cooking Time: 75 Min
Ingredients:

- 1 pound parsnips, peeled and cut into chunks /450g
- 3 cans chopped mussels, drained, liquid reserved /180g
- 1½ cups heavy cream /375ml
- 2 cups oyster crackers /260g
- ¼ cup white wine /62.5ml
- ¼ cup finely grated Pecorino Romano cheese/32.5g
- 1 cup clam juice /130g
- 2 thick pancetta slices, cut into thirds
- 1 bay leaf
- 2 celery stalks; chopped
- 1 medium onion; chopped
- 1 tbsp flour /15g
- 2 tbsps chopped fresh chervil/30g
- 2 tbsps melted ghee /30g
- ½ tsp garlic powder /2.5g
- 1 tsp salt; divided /5g
- 1 tsp dried rosemary /5g

Directions:

1. To preheat the Foodi, close the crisping lid and Choose Air Crisp; adjust the temperature to 375°F or 191°C and the time to 2 minutes; press Start. In a bowl, pour in the oyster crackers. Drizzle with the melted ghee, add the cheese, garlic powder, and ½ tsp or 2.5g of salt. Toss to coat the crackers. Transfer to the crisping basket.

2. Once the pot is ready, open the pressure lid and fix the basket in the pot. Close the lid and Choose Air Crisp; adjust the temperature to 375°F or 191°C and the cook time to 6 minutes; press Start.

3. After 3 minutes, carefully open the lid and mix the crackers with a spoon. Close the lid and resume cooking until crisp and lightly browned. Take out the basket and set aside to cool.

4. On the pot, choose Sear/Sauté and adjust to Medium. Press Start. Add the pancetta and cook for 5 minutes, turning once or twice, until crispy.

5. Remove the pancetta to a paper towel-lined plate to drain fat; set aside.

6. Sauté the celery and onion in the pancetta grease for 1 minute or until the vegetables start softening. Mix the flour into the vegetables to coat evenly and pour the wine over the veggies. Cook for about 1 minute or until reduced by about one-third.

7. Pour in the clam juice, the reserved mussel liquid, parsnips, remaining salt, rosemary, and bay leaf. Seal the pressure lid, choose Pressure; adjust the pressure to High and the cook time to 4 minutes. Press Start.

8. After cooking, perform a natural pressure release for 5 minutes. Stir in the mussels and heavy cream. Choose Sear/Sauté and adjust to Medium. Press Start to simmer to the chowder and heat the mussels. Carefully remove and discard the bay leaf after.

9. Spoon the soup into bowls and crumble the pancetta over the top. Garnish with the chervil and a handful of oyster crackers, serving the remaining crackers on the side.

Citrus Glazed Halibut

Servings: 4
Cooking Time: 10 Minutes

Ingredients:

- Nonstick cooking spray
- 1 onion, chopped
- 1 clove garlic, chopped fine
- 4 halibut steaks
- ½ tsp salt
- ¼ tsp lemon-pepper
- ½ cup fresh orange juice
- 1 tbsp. fresh lemon juice
- 2 tbsp. fresh parsley, chopped fine

Directions:

1. Spray the cooking pot with cooking spray. Set to sauté on medium heat.
2. Add the onion and garlic and cook 2-3 minutes until onion starts to soften.
3. Add the halibut and season with salt and pepper. Drizzle the orange and lemon juices over the fish and sprinkle with parsley.
4. Add the lid and reduce heat to med-low. Cook 10-12 minutes until fish flakes easily with a fork. Serve immediately.

Nutrition:

- InfoCalories 131,Total Fat 2g,Total Carbs 6g,Protein 22g,Sodium 370mg.

Tuna & Avocado Patties

Servings: 6
Cooking Time: 20 Minutes

Ingredients:

- Nonstick cooking spray
- 1 avocado, peeled & pitted
- 10 oz. Albacore tuna, drained
- ¼ cup whole wheat bread crumbs
- ¼ cup red onion, chopped fine
- 2 tbsp. cilantro, chopped
- 1 tbsp. fresh lime juice
- 1 tsp hot sauce
- ½ tsp garlic powder
- ½ tsp salt
- 1 egg

Directions:

1. Spray the fryer basket with cooking spray.
2. In a large bowl, mash the avocado. Add the remaining ingredients and mix well. Form into 6 patties.
3. Place the patties in the basket. Add the tender-crisp lid and set to air fry on 400°F. Cook patties 15 minutes or until crisp and cooked through, turning over halfway through cooking time. Serve.

Nutrition:

- InfoCalories 102,Total Fat 5g,Total Carbs 6g,Protein 10g,Sodium 269mg.

Sesame Tuna Steaks

Servings: 4
Cooking Time: 10 Minutes
Ingredients:

- Nonstick cooking spray
- 2 tsp sesame oil
- 1 clove garlic, chopped fine
- 4 tuna steaks
- 1/8 tsp salt
- ½ tsp pepper
- ½ cup sesame seeds

Directions:

1. Place the rack in the cooking pot and spray it with cooking spray.
2. In a small bowl combine the oil and garlic. Rub it on both sides of the fish. Season with salt and pepper.
3. Place the sesame seeds in a shallow dish. Press the fish in the sesame seeds to coat completely. Place them on the rack.
4. Add the tender-crisp lid and set to roast on 350°F. Cook 8-10 minutes, turning over halfway through cooking time, until fish flakes with a fork. Serve immediately.

Nutrition:

- InfoCalories 263,Total Fat 14g,Total Carbs 3g,Protein 32g,Sodium 60mg.

Teriyaki Salmon

Servings: 4
Cooking Time: 15 Minutes
Ingredients:

- ½ cup brown sugar
- ½ cup soy sauce, low sodium
- ¼ cup cider vinegar
- 2 cloves garlic, chopped fine
- ¼ tsp pepper
- ½ tsp salt
- ½ tsp sesame oil
- 1 tbsp. water
- 1 tbsp. cornstarch
- 4 salmon filets
- 2 tbsp. green onions, sliced thin
- 2 tbsp. sesame seeds

Directions:

1. Set to sauté on medium heat. Add the brown sugar, soy sauce, vinegar, garlic, pepper, salt, and oil to the cooking pot. Stir until smooth.
2. In a small bowl, whisk together the water and cornstarch until smooth. Slowly whisk it into the sauce. Bring to a boil and cook 1-2 minutes until it starts to thicken. Reserve ¼ cup sauce.
3. Set cooker to bake on 400°F. Add the salmon to the pot and spoon sauce over the top. Add the tender-crisp lid and bake 15 minutes until salmon is firm to the touch but flakes easily.
4. Transfer salmon to serving plates and brush tops with reserved sauce. Garnish with green onion and sesame seeds and serve.

Nutrition:

- InfoCalories 309,Total Fat 14g,Total Carbs 34g,Protein 38g,Sodium 2090mg.

Shrimp & Zoodles

Servings: 6
Cooking Time:x
Ingredients:

- 2 tbsp. olive oil, divided
- 1 lb. shrimp, peel & devein
- 2 cloves garlic, chopped fine
- 3 zucchini, peel & spiralize
- ½ tsp salt
- ¼ tsp pepper
- ½ tsp red pepper flakes
- 1 tbsp. fresh lemon juice
- 1 cup cherry tomatoes, halved

Directions:

1. Add 1 tablespoon oil to the cooking pot and set to sauté on medium heat. Add shrimp and cook until pink 2-3 minutes. Transfer to a plate and cover.
2. Add remaining oil to the pot with the garlic. Cook 1 minute, stirring.
3. Add the zucchini, salt, pepper, red pepper flakes, lemon juice, and tomatoes and toss to combine. Cook until zucchini is tender, about 5-7 minutes, stirring occasionally.
4. Place shrimp on top of the zucchini mixture, cover, and turn off heat. Let sit for 1 minute. Serve immediately.

Nutrition:

- InfoCalories 153,Total Fat 7g,Total Carbs 5g,Protein 19g,Sodium 283mg.

Speedy Clams Pomodoro

Servings: 4
Cooking Time: 10 Minutes
Ingredients:

- 2 dozen clams
- 14 ½ oz. stewed tomatoes, chopped & undrained
- ¼ cup dry white wine
- 2 tbsp. fresh basil, chopped
- ¼ tsp pepper
- 1 lemon, cut in wedges

Directions:

1. Set cooker to sauté on med-high heat.
2. Add all the ingredients to the cooking pot and stir to mix.
3. Add the lid and bring mixture to a boil. Reduce heat to low and simmer 6-8 minutes or until the clams open.
4. Discard any unopened clams and serve immediately with lemon wedges.

Nutrition:

- InfoCalories 123,Total Fat 1g,Total Carbs 12g,Protein 14g,Sodium 715mg.

Crab Cake Casserole

Servings:8
Cooking Time: 17 Minutes

Ingredients:

- 2 tablespoons canola oil
- 1 large onion, chopped
- 2 celery stalks, chopped
- 1 red bell pepper, chopped
- 1½ cups basmati rice, rinsed
- 2 cups chicken stock
- ¼ cup mayonnaise
- ¼ cup Dijon mustard
- 3 cans lump crab meat
- 1 cup shredded Cheddar cheese, divided
- 1 sleeve butter crackers, crumbled

Directions:

1. Select SEAR/SAUTÉ and set to HI. Select START/STOP to begin. Let preheat for 5 minutes.

2. Add the oil. Once hot, add the onion, celery, and bell pepper and stir. Cook for 5 minutes, stirring occasionally.

3. Stir in the rice and chicken stock. Assemble pressure lid, making sure the pressure release valve is in the SEAL position.

4. Select PRESSURE and set to HI. Set time to 2 minutes. Select START/STOP to begin.

5. When pressure cooking is complete, allow pressure to naturally release for 10 minutes. After 10 minutes, quick release any remaining pressure by moving the pressure release valve to the VENT position. Carefully remove lid when unit has finished releasing pressure.

6. Stir in the mayonnaise, mustard, crab, and ½ cup of Cheddar cheese. Top evenly with the crackers, then top with remaining ½ cup of cheese. Close crisping lid.

7. Select BAKE/ROAST, set temperature to 350°F, and set time to 10 minutes. Select START/STOP to begin.

8. When cooking is complete, open lid and serve immediately.

Nutrition:

- InfoCalories: 448,Total Fat: 25g,Sodium: 819mg,Carbohydrates: 46g,Protein: 22g.

Baked Cod Casserole

Servings: 6
Cooking Time: 20 Minutes

Ingredients:

- Nonstick cooking spray
- 1 lb. mushrooms, chopped
- 1 onion, chopped
- ½ cup fresh parsley, chopped
- ½ tsp salt, divided
- ½ tsp pepper, divided
- 6 cod fillets
- ¾ cup dry white wine
- ¾ cup plain bread crumbs
- 2 tbsp. butter, melted
- 1 cup Swiss cheese, grated

Directions:

1. Spray the cooking pot with cooking spray.
2. In a medium bowl, combine mushrooms, onion, parsley, ¼ teaspoon salt, and ¼ teaspoon pepper and mix well. Spread evenly on the bottom of the cooking pot.
3. Place the fish on top of the mushroom mixture and pour the wine over them.
4. In a separate medium bowl, combine remaining ingredients and mix well. Sprinkle over the fish.
5. Add the tender-crisp lid and set to bake on 450°F. Bake 15-20 minutes or until golden brown and fish flakes easily with a fork. Serve immediately.

Nutrition:

- InfoCalories 284,Total Fat 10g,Total Carbs 16g,Protein 27g,Sodium 693mg.

Shrimp & Asparagus Risotto

Servings: 4

Cooking Time: 25 Minutes

Ingredients:

- 1 tbsp. butter
- ½ onion, chopped fine
- 1 clove garlic, chopped fine
- 1 cup Arborio rice
- 5 cups water, divided
- 1 cup clam juice
- 1 tbsp. olive oil
- ½ lb. small shrimp, peeled & deveined
- ½ bunch asparagus, cut in 1-inch pieces
- ¼ cup parmesan cheese

Directions:

1. Add butter to cooking pot and set to sauté on medium heat. Once butter melts, add onion and garlic and cook 5 minutes, stirring frequently.

2. Add the rice and stir to coat with butter mixture. Transfer mixture to a 1-quart baking dish.

3. Pour 1 cup water and clam juice over rice mixture and cover tightly with foil.

4. Pour 2 cups water in the cooking pot and add the rack. Place the rice mixture on the rack, secure the lid and set to pressure cooking on high. Set timer for 10 minutes.

5. When timer goes off release the pressure quickly and remove the baking dish carefully. Drain out any remaining water.

6. Set the cooker back to sauté on med-high and heat the oil. Add the shrimp and asparagus and cook, stirring, just until shrimp start to turn pink.

7. Add the shrimp and asparagus to the rice and stir to mix well. Recover tightly with foil. Pour 2 cups water back in the pot and add the rack.

8. Place the rice mixture back on the rack and secure the lid. Set to pressure cooking on high and set the timer for 4 minutes.

9. When the timer goes off, release the pressure quickly. Remove the foil and stir. Serve immediately sprinkled with parmesan cheese.

Nutrition:

- InfoCalories 362,Total Fat 11g,Total Carbs 45g,Protein 20g,Sodium 623mg.

Arroz Con Cod

Servings: 4

Cooking Time: 30 Minutes

Ingredients:

- ¼ cup olive oil
- 2 tbsp. garlic, chopped
- ½ cup red onion, chopped
- ½ cup red bell pepper, chopped
- ½ cup green bell pepper, chopped
- 2 cups long grain rice
- 3 tbsp. tomato paste
- 2 tsp turmeric
- 2 tbsp. cumin
- ½ tsp salt
- ¼ tsp pepper
- 4 cups chicken broth
- 1 bay leaf
- 1 lb. cod, cut in bite-size pieces
- ½ cup peas, cooked
- 4 tbsp. pimento, chopped
- 4 tsp cilantro, chopped

Directions:

1. Add the oil to the cooking pot and set to sauté on med-high.
2. Add the garlic, onion, and peppers, and cook, stirring frequently for 2 minutes.
3. Stir in rice, tomato paste, and seasonings, and cook another 2 minutes.
4. Add the broth and bay leaf and bring to a boil. Reduce heat, cover, and let simmer 5 minutes.
5. Add the fish, recover the pot and cook 15-20 minutes until all the liquid is absorbed. Turn off the cooker and let sit for 5 minutes.
6. To serve: spoon onto plates and top with cooked peas, pimento and cilantro.

Nutrition:

- InfoCalories 282,Total Fat 15g,Total Carbs 35g,Protein 4g,Sodium 1249mg.

Flounder Oreganata

Servings: 4

Cooking Time: 15 Minutes

Ingredients:

- 1/3 cup rolled oats
- ¼ cup panko bread crumbs
- 2 cloves garlic, chopped fine
- 2 tbsp. fresh parsley, chopped, divided
- ½ tsp oregano
- 4 tsp fresh lemon juice
- 1 tsp lemon zest
- 1 tbsp. olive oil
- 1 tsp salt, divided
- ½ tsp pepper
- 4 flounder fillets
- Lemon wedges

Directions:

1. Place the rack in the cooking pot and top with a piece of parchment paper.
2. Add the oats to a food processor and pulse until they are finely ground.
3. In a small bowl, combine oats, bread crumbs, garlic, 1 ½ tablespoons parsley, oregano, lemon juice, zest, oil and ½ tsp salt.
4. Lay the fish on the parchment paper and season with salt and pepper. Spoon bread crumb mixture over the fish, pressing lightly.
5. Add the tender-crisp lid and set to bake on 450°F. Bake 10-12 minutes until topping is golden brown and fish flakes easily with a fork. Serve garnished with parsley and lemon wedges.

Nutrition:

- InfoCalories 261,Total Fat 9g,Total Carbs 14g,Protein 30g,Sodium 1459mg.

Salmon Kale Meal

Servings: 4

Cooking Time: 4 Minutes

Ingredients:

- 1 lemon, juiced
- 2 salmon fillets
- 1/4 cup extra virgin olive oil
- 1 teaspoon Dijon mustard
- 4 cups kale, sliced, ribs removed
- 1 teaspoon salt
- 1 avocado, diced
- 1 cup pomegranate seeds
- 1 cup walnuts, toasted
- 1 cup goat parmesan cheese, shredded

Directions:

1. Season salmon with salt and keep it on the side.
2. Place a trivet in your Ninja Foodi.
3. Place salmon over the trivet.
4. Release pressure naturally over 10 minutes.
5. Transfer salmon to a serving platter.
6. Take a suitable and stir in kale, season with salt.
7. Season kale with dressing and add diced avocado, pomegranate seeds, walnuts and cheese.
8. Toss and serve with the fish.
9. Enjoy.

Nutrition:

- InfoCalories: 234; Fat: 14g; Carbohydrates: 12g; Protein: 16g

Crabmeat With Broccoli Risotto

Servings: 4

Cooking Time: 80 Min

Ingredients:

- 1 pound broccoli, cut into florets and chopped into 1-inch pieces /450g
- 8 ounces lump crabmeat /240g
- 1 small onion; chopped (about ½ cup) /65g
- 2 cups vegetable stock /500ml
- ⅓ cup grated Pecorino Romano cheese/44g
- 1 cup short grain rice /130g
- ⅓ cup white wine /88ml
- 1 tbsp olive oil /15ml
- 1 tsp salt; divided /5g
- 2 tbsps ghee /30g

Directions:

1. Preheat your Foodi by closing the crisping lid. Choose Air Crisp; adjust the temperature to 375°F or 191°C and the time to 2 minutes. Press Start. Add the broccoli in the crisping basket and drizzle with the olive oil. Season with ½ tsp of salt and toss.

2. Put the basket in the inner pot. Close the crisping lid; choose Air Crisp, adjust the temperature to 375°F or 191°C and the cook time to 10 minutes. Press Start.

3. After 5 minutes, open the lid and stir the broccoli, then resume cooking. When done cooking, take out the basket and set aside.

4. Choose Sear/Sauté and adjust to Medium. Press Start and melt the ghee. Add and sauté the onion for 5 minutes until softened.

5. Stir in the rice and cook for 1 minute. Add the wine and cook for 2 to 3 minutes, stirring frequently, until the liquid has almost completely evaporated.

6. Pour in vegetable stock and the remaining salt. Stir to combine. Seal the pressure lid, choose Pressure, adjust the pressure to High, and the cook time to 8 minutes. Press Start.

7. After cooking, perform a quick pressure release and carefully open the pressure lid. Gently stir in the crabmeat, and cheese. Taste and adjust the seasoning. Serve immediately.

Chapter 6 Snacks, Appetizers & Sides

Teriyaki Chicken Wings

Servings: 6

Cooking Time: 30 Min

Ingredients:

- 2 lb. chicken wings /900g
- 1 cup teriyaki sauce /250ml
- 1 tbsp honey /15ml
- 2 tbsp cornstarch 30g
- 2 tbsp cold water /30ml
- 1 tsp finely ground black pepper /5g
- 1 tsp sesame seeds /5g

Directions:

1. In the pot, combine honey, teriyaki sauce and black pepper until the honey dissolves completely; toss in chicken to coat. Seal the pressure lid, choose Pressure, set to High, and set the timer to 10 minutes. Press Start.
2. When ready, release the pressure quickly. Transfer chicken wings to a platter. Mix cold water with the cornstarch.
3. Press Sear/Sauté and stir in cornstarch slurry into the sauce and cook for 3 to 5 minutes until thickened. Top the chicken with thickened sauce. Add a garnish of sesame seeds, and serve.

Honey-garlic Chicken Wings

Servings:4

Cooking Time: 43 Minutes

Ingredients:

- 2 pounds fresh chicken wings
- ¾ cup potato starch
- Cooking spray
- ¼ cup unsalted butter
- 4 tablespoons minced garlic
- ¼ cup honey
- ¼ teaspoon sea salt

Directions:

1. Insert Cook & Crisp Basket into pot and close crisping lid. Select AIR CRISP, set temperature to 390°F, and set time to 5 minutes. Select START/STOP to begin preheating.
2. Pat the chicken wings dry. In a large bowl, toss the chicken wings with potato starch until evenly coated.
3. Once unit has preheated, place the wings in the basket. Close lid.
4. Select AIR CRISP, set temperature to 390°F, and set time to 30 minutes. Select START/STOP to begin.
5. After 15 minutes, open lid, then lift the basket and shake the wings. Coat with cooking spray. Lower basket back into the pot. Close lid and continue cooking until the wings reach your desired crispiness.
6. Cooking is complete when the internal temperature of the meat reads at least 165°F on a food thermometer.
7. Remove basket from pot. Cover with aluminum foil to keep warm.
8. Select SEAR/SAUTÉ and set to MD:LO. Select START/STOP to begin.
9. Add the butter and garlic and sauté until fragrant, about 3 minutes. Add the honey and salt and simmer for about 10 minutes, adding water as needed to thin out the sauce.
10. Place the wings in a large bowl. Drizzle with the sauce and toss the chicken wings to coat. Serve.

Nutrition:

- InfoCalories: 654,Total Fat: 33g,Sodium: 302mg,Carbohydrates: 53g,Protein: 39g.

Cheesy Stuffed Mushroom

Servings: 7
Cooking Time: 7 Minutes
Ingredients:

- 12 ounces Parmesan cheese
- 7 mushroom caps
- 2 teaspoons minced garlic
- ¼ sour cream
- 1 teaspoon butter
- 1 teaspoon ground white pepper
- 2 teaspoons oregano

Directions:

1. Mix the minced garlic, sour cream, ground white pepper, and oregano, and stir the mixture.
2. Add grated parmesan to the minced garlic mixture.
3. Blend the mixture until smooth.
4. Stuff the mushrooms with the cheese mixture and place the dish in the Ninja Foodi's insert.
5. Set the Ninja Foodi's insert to "Pressure" mode, add butter, and close the Ninja Foodi's lid.
6. Cook the dish for 7 minutes.
7. Once done, remove it from the Ninja Foodi's insert, let it rest briefly, and serve.

Nutrition:

- InfoCalories: 203; Fat: 7.6g; Carbohydrates: 8.35g; Protein: 8g

White Bean Hummus

Servings: 8
Cooking Time: 8 Hours
Ingredients:

- 2 cups small white beans, soaked overnight
- 2 tbsp. pine nuts
- 1 tsp lemon zest, grated
- 1 tbsp. fresh lemon juice
- ¼ tsp garlic powder
- ¼ tsp salt

Directions:

1. Place beans with just enough water to cover them in the cooking pot. Add the lid and set to slow cooker function on low heat. Cook 8 hours, or until beans are tender.
2. Drain the beans, reserving some of the cooking liquid. Place beans in a food processor.
3. Wipe the cooking pot and set to sauté on low heat. Add the pine nuts and cook, stirring frequently, until lightly browned.
4. Add the lemon zest and juice, garlic powder, and salt to the beans. Pulse until almost smooth. If hummus is too thick, add reserved cooking liquid, a tablespoon at a time, until desired consistency.
5. Transfer hummus to a serving bowl and sprinkle with pine nuts. Serve.

Nutrition:

- InfoCalories 169,Total Fat 1g,Total Carbs 31g,Protein 12g,Sodium 81mg.

Beef Chicken Meatloaf

Servings: 9
Cooking Time: 40 Minutes
Ingredients:

- 2 cups ground beef
- 1 cup ground chicken
- 2 eggs
- 1 tablespoon salt
- 1 teaspoon black pepper
- ½ teaspoon paprika
- 1 tablespoon butter
- 1 teaspoon cilantro, chopped
- 1 tablespoon basil
- ¼ cup fresh dill, chopped

Directions:

1. Combine the ground chicken and ground beef together in a mixing bowl.
2. Add egg, salt, black pepper, paprika, butter, and cilantro.
3. Add the basil and dill and add it to the ground meat mixture and stir using your hands.
4. Place the meat mixture on aluminium foil, shape into a loaf and wrap it.
5. Place it in the Ninja Foodi's insert. Close the Ninja Foodi's lid and cook the dish in the" Sauté" mode for 40 minutes.
6. Once done, remove the meatloaf from the Ninja Foodi's insert and let it rest.
7. Remove from the foil, slice it, and serve.

Nutrition:

- InfoCalories: 173; Fat: 11.5g; Carbohydrates: 0.81g; Protein: 16g

Zucchini Egg Tots

Servings: 8
Cooking Time: 9 Minutes
Ingredients:

- 2 medium zucchinis
- 1 egg
- 1 teaspoon salt
- ½ teaspoon baking soda
- 1 teaspoon lemon juice
- 1 teaspoon basil
- 1 tablespoon oregano
- ⅓ cup oatmeal flour
- 1 tablespoon olive oil
- 1 teaspoon minced garlic
- 1 tablespoon butter

Directions:

1. Wash the zucchini and grate it. Beat the egg in a suitable mixing bowl and blend it using a whisk.
2. Add the baking soda, lemon juice, basil, oregano, and flour to the egg mixture.
3. Stir it carefully until smooth. Combine the grated zucchini and egg mixture together.
4. Knead the dough until smooth. Mix olive oil with minced garlic together.
5. Set the Ninja Foodi's insert to" Sauté" mode.
6. Add butter and transfer the mixture to the Ninja Foodi's insert. Melt the mixture.
7. Make the small tots from the zucchini dough and place them in the melted butter mixture.
8. Sauté the dish for 3 minutes on each side.
9. Once the zucchini tots are cooked, remove them from the Ninja Foodi's insert and serve.

Nutrition:

- InfoCalories: 64; Fat: 4.4g; Carbohydrates: 4.35g; Protein: 2g

Rosemary Potato Fries

Servings: 4

Cooking Time: 30 Min

Ingredients:

- 4 russet potatoes, cut into sticks
- 2 garlic cloves, crushed
- 2 tbsp butter, melted /30ml
- 1 tsp fresh rosemary; chopped /5g
- Salt and pepper, to taste

Directions:

1. Add butter, garlic, salt, and pepper to a bowl; toss until the sticks are well-coated. Lay the potato sticks into the Ninja Foodi's basket. Close the crisping lid and cook for 15 minutes at 370 °F or 188°C. Shake the potatoes every 5 minutes.
2. Once ready, check to ensure the fries are golden and crispy all over if not, return them to cook for a few minutes.
3. Divide standing up between metal cups lined with nonstick baking paper, and serve sprinkled with rosemary.

Herb Roasted Mixed Nuts

Servings: 12

Cooking Time: 15 Minutes

Ingredients:

- ½ cup pecan halves
- ½ cup raw cashews
- ½ cup walnut halves
- ½ cup hazelnuts
- ½ cup Brazil nuts
- ½ cup raw almonds
- 1 tbsp. fresh rosemary, chopped
- 1 tbsp. fresh thyme, chopped
- ½ tbsp. fresh parsley, chopped
- 1 tsp garlic granules
- ½ tsp paprika
- ½ tsp salt
- ¼ tsp pepper
- ½ tbsp. olive oil

Directions:

1. Combine all ingredients in a large bowl and toss to coat thoroughly.
2. Pour the nuts in the fryer basket and place in the cooking pot. Add the tender-crisp lid and select air fry on 375°F. Cook 10 minutes, then stir the nuts around.
3. Cook another 5-10 minutes, stirring every few minutes and checking to make sure they don't burn. Serve warm.

Nutrition:

- InfoCalories 229,Total Fat 21g,Total Carbs 7g,Protein 5g,Sodium 99mg.

Bacon Wrapped Scallops

Servings: 8
Cooking Time: 10 Minutes

Ingredients:

- 1/3 cup ketchup
- 2 tbsp. vinegar
- 1 tbsp. brown sugar
- ¼ tsp hot pepper sauce
- 13 slices turkey bacon, cut in half
- 1 lb. scallops, rinse & pat dry
- Nonstick cooking spray

Directions:

1. In a large bowl, whisk together ketchup, vinegar, brown sugar, and hot pepper sauce until smooth.
2. Wrap each scallop with a piece of bacon and use a toothpick to secure. Add to the sauce and toss to coat. Cover and refrigerate 20 minutes.
3. Place the rack in the cooking pot. Spray a small baking sheet with cooking spray. Working in batches, place scallops in a single layer on the tray and place on the rack.
4. Add the tender-crisp lid and set to air fry on 450°F. Cook scallops 4-5 minutes, then flip over and cook another 4-5 minutes or until cooked through. Serve immediately.

Nutrition:

- InfoCalories 100,Total Fat 2g,Total Carbs 6g,Protein 13g,Sodium 525mg.

Strawberry Snack Bars

Servings: 16
Cooking Time: 30 Minutes

Ingredients:

- Butter flavored cooking spray
- 1 cup butter, soft
- 2 oz. stevia
- 1 tbsp. sour cream, reduced fat
- 1 egg
- 1 cup flour
- 1 cup whole wheat flour
- 1 cup strawberry jam, sugar free
- 1 tbsp. brown sugar
- 2 tbsp. walnuts, chopped

Directions:

1. Spray an 8-inch square pan with cooking spray.
2. In a medium bowl, beat butter and Stevia until creamy.
3. Beat in sour cream and egg until combined.
4. Stir in both flours, ½ cup at a time, until mixture forms a soft dough.
5. Press half the dough in the bottom of the prepared pan. Spread the jam over the top. Then spread the other half of the dough gently over the top. Sprinkle the brown sugar and nuts over the top.
6. Place the rack in the cooking pot and place the pan on it. Add the tender-crisp lid and set to bake on 375°F. Bake 25-30 minutes until bubbly and golden brown.
7. Transfer to wire rack to cool before cutting.

Nutrition:

- InfoCalories 195,Total Fat 13g,Total Carbs 22g,Protein 3g,Sodium 97mg.

Dill Butter

Servings: 7
Cooking Time: 5 Minutes
Ingredients:

- 1 cup butter
- 1 teaspoon minced garlic
- 1 teaspoon dried oregano
- 1 teaspoon dried cilantro
- 1 tablespoon dried dill
- 1 teaspoon salt
- ½ teaspoon black pepper

Directions:

1. Set "Sauté" mode and place butter inside the Ninja Foodi's insert.
2. Add minced garlic, dried oregano, dried cilantro, butter, dried dill, salt, and black pepper.
3. Stir the mixture well and sauté it for 4-5 minutes or until the butter is melted.
4. Then switch off the cooker and stir the butter well.
5. Transfer the butter mixture into the butter mould and freeze it.

Nutrition:

- InfoCalories: 235; Fat: 26.3g; Carbohydrates: 0.6g; Protein: 0.4g

South Of The Border Corn Dip

Servings: 8
Cooking Time: 2 Hours
Ingredients:

- 33 oz. corn with chilies
- 10 oz. tomatoes & green chilies, diced
- 8 oz. cream cheese, cubed
- ½ cup cheddar cheese, grated
- ¼ cup green onions, chopped
- ½ tsp garlic, diced fine
- ½ tsp chili powder

Directions:

1. Place all ingredients in the cooking pot and stir to mix.
2. Add the lid and set to slow cooking function on low heat. Set timer for 2 hours. Stir occasionally.
3. Dip is done when all the cheese is melted and it's bubbly. Stir well, then transfer to serving bowl and serve warm.

Nutrition:

- InfoCalories 225,Total Fat 13g,Total Carbs 24g,Protein 7g,Sodium 710mg.

Almond Lover's Bars

Servings: 20
Cooking Time: 30 Minutes
Ingredients:

- 2 cups almond flour, sifted
- 1 ½ cups flour
- 1 tsp baking powder
- ½ tsp salt
- 10 tbsp. butter, soft
- 1 cup sugar
- 2 eggs
- 2 tsp vanilla
- 1 tbsp. powdered sugar

Directions:

1. Line an 8-inch square baking dish with parchment paper.
2. In a medium bowl, whisk together both flours, baking powder, and salt.
3. In a large bowl, beat butter and sugar until creamy.
4. Beat in eggs and vanilla. Then stir in dry ingredients until combined. Press firmly in prepared pan.
5. Place the rack in the cooking pot and place the pan on it. Add the tender-crisp lid and set to bake on 325°F. Bake 25-30 minutes until lightly browned and the bars pass the toothpick test.
6. Let cool before cutting into bars. Sprinkle with powdered sugar before serving.

Nutrition:

- InfoCalories 207,Total Fat 11g,Total Carbs 23g,Protein 3g,Sodium 83mg.

Parmesan Stuffed Mushrooms

Servings: 5
Cooking Time: 15 Minutes
Ingredients:

- 1 lb. button mushrooms, wash & remove stems
- 2 tbsp. olive oil, divided
- ¼ cup parmesan cheese, fat free
- 2 cloves garlic, diced fine
- ¼ cup cream cheese, fat free, soft
- ¼ cup whole wheat panko bread crumbs

Directions:

1. Place the rack in the cooking pot and top with a piece of parchment paper.
2. Brush the mushrooms with 1 tablespoon oil.
3. In a small bowl, combine parmesan, garlic, and cream cheese until smooth. Spoon 1 teaspoon of the mixture into each mushroom. Place mushrooms on parchment paper.
4. In a separate small bowl, stir together bread crumbs and remaining oil. Sprinkle over tops of mushrooms.
5. Add the tender-crisp lid and select bake on 375°F. Cook mushrooms 15 minutes, or until tops are nicely browned and mushrooms are tender. Serve immediately.

Nutrition:

- InfoCalories 121,Total Fat 6g,Total Carbs 10g,Protein 7g,Sodium 191mg.

Asian Chicken Nuggets

Servings: X

Cooking Time: 20 Minutes

Ingredients:

- 1 lb. chicken breasts, boneless, skinless & cut in 1-inch pieces
- 1 tsp salt
- ½ tsp pepper
- 2 eggs
- 1 cup Panko bread crumbs
- ¼ cup lite soy sauce
- ¼ cup honey
- 4 cloves garlic, diced fine
- 2 tbsp. hoisin sauce
- 1 tablespoon freshly grated ginger
- 1 tablespoon Sriracha
- 2 green onions, sliced thin
- 2 tsp sesame seeds

Directions:

1. Place the rack in the cooking pot and top with a sheet of parchment paper.
2. Sprinkle the chicken with salt and pepper.
3. In a shallow dish, beat the eggs.
4. Place the bread crumbs in a separate shallow dish. Working in batches, dip the chicken first in the eggs then bread crumbs, pressing to coat the chicken well.
5. Place the chicken on the parchment paper in a single layer. Add the tender-crisp lid and select air fry on 400 °F. Bake the chicken 10-15 minutes until golden brown and cooked through, turning over halfway through cooking time. Transfer to serving plate and keep warm.
6. Set the cooker to sauté on med-high heat. Add the soy sauce, honey, garlic, hoisin, ginger, and Sriracha, stir to combine. Cook, stirring frequently, until sauce thickens, about 2 minutes.
7. Add chicken and toss to coat. Serve immediately garnished with green onions and sesame seeds.

Nutrition:

- InfoCalories 304,Total Fat 7g,Total Carbs 27g,Protein 32g,Sodium 1149mg.

Wrapped Asparagus In Bacon

Servings: 6
Cooking Time: 30 Min
Ingredients:

- 1 lb. bacon; sliced /450g
- 1 lb. asparagus spears, trimmed /450g
- ½ cup Parmesan cheese, grated /65g
- Cooking spray
- Salt and pepper, to taste

Directions:

1. Place the bacon slices out on a work surface, top each one with one asparagus spear and half of the cheese. Wrap the bacon around the asparagus.
2. Line the Ninja Foodi basket with parchment paper. Arrange the wraps into the basket, scatter over the remaining cheese, season with salt and black pepper, and spray with cooking spray. Close the crisping lid and cook for 8 to 10 minutes on Roast mode at 370 °F or 188°C. If necessary, work in batches. Serve hot!

Cheesy Bacon Brussel Sprouts

Servings: 6
Cooking Time: 15 Minutes
Ingredients:

- Nonstick cooking spray
- 3 slices turkey bacon, chopped
- 2 tsp olive oil
- 1 lb. Brussels sprouts, trimmed & cut in half
- 2 cloves garlic, diced fine
- ¼ cup water
- 3 oz. goat cheese, soft
- 2 tbsp. skim milk
- 1 tbsp. parmesan cheese
- ¼ tsp salt
- ¼ tsp pepper
- 1 tsp paprika

Directions:

1. Spray the cooking pot with cooking spray. Set to sauté on med-high heat.
2. Add bacon and cook until crisp, transfer to paper-towel line plate.
3. Add oil and let it get hot. Add Brussel sprouts and cook, stirring frequently, 5 minutes or until they start to brown.
4. Add water, cover and cook another 5 minutes or until fork-tender. Drain any water from the pot.
5. Add goat cheese, milk, parmesan, salt, and pepper. Cook, stirring frequently, until cheese has melted.
6. Stir in bacon and cook until heated through. Sprinkle with paprika and serve.

Nutrition:

- InfoCalories 106,Total Fat 6g,Total Carbs 8g,Protein 7g,Sodium 274mg.

Mexican Street Corn Queso Dip

Servings:8
Cooking Time: 20 Minutes

Ingredients:

- 1 package cream cheese, quartered
- 6 ounces cotija cheese, crumbled, 2 ounces reserved for topping
- 1 can fire-roasted tomatoes with chiles
- ½ cup mayonnaise
- Zest of 2 limes
- Juice of 2 limes
- 2 packages shredded Mexican cheese blend, divided
- 1 garlic clove, grated
- 1 can cream corn
- 1 cup frozen corn
- Kosher salt
- Freshly ground black pepper

Directions:

1. Pour the cream cheese, 4 ounces of cotija cheese, tomatoes with chiles, mayonnaise, lime zest and juice, one 8-ounce package Mexican cheese blend, garlic, cream corn, and frozen corn in the pot. Season with salt and pepper and stir. Close crisping lid.
2. Select BAKE/ROAST, set temperature to 375°F, and set time to 20 minutes. Select START/STOP to begin.
3. After 10 minutes, open lid and sprinkle the dip with the remaining 2 ounces of cotija cheese and remaining 8-ounce package of Mexican blend cheese. Close crisping lid and continue cooking.
4. When cooking is complete, the cheese will be melted and the dip hot and bubbling at the edges. Open lid and let the dip cool for 5 to 10 minutes before serving. Serve topped with chopped cilantro, hot sauce, and chili powder, if desired.

Nutrition:

- InfoCalories: 538,Total Fat: 45g,Sodium: 807mg,Carbohydrates: 18g,Protein: 20g.

Brie Spread With Cherries & Pistachios

Servings: 10
Cooking Time: 3 Hours

Ingredients:

- ½ cup dried cherries, chopped
- ¼ cup cherry preserves
- 1 tbsp. Cognac
- 2 8 oz. wheels Brie cheese
- ½ cup pistachio nuts, toasted & chopped

Directions:

1. In a small bowl, combine cherries, preserves, and cognac, mix well.
2. Place on wheel of Brie in the cooking pot. Pour half the cherry mixture over the top. Repeat layers one more time.
3. Add the lid and select slow cooking function on low heat. Set timer for 3 hours.
4. Cook until cheese is soft, but not melted. Transfer to a serving plate and sprinkle with toasted pistachios. Serve warm.

Nutrition:

- InfoCalories 224,Total Fat 15g,Total Carbs 10g,Protein 11g,Sodium 290mg.

Parmesan Breadsticks

Servings: 8
Cooking Time: 10 Minutes
Ingredients:

- 1 teaspoon baking powder
- ½ teaspoon Erythritol
- ½ teaspoon salt
- 1 cup of warm water
- 2 cups almond flour
- 5 ounces Parmesan
- 1 tablespoon olive oil
- 1 teaspoon onion powder
- 1 teaspoon basil

Directions:

1. Combine the baking powder, Erythritol, and warm water in a mixing bowl.
2. Stir the mixture well. Add the almond flour, onion powder, salt, and basil.
3. Knead the dough until smooth. Separate dough into 10 pieces and make the long logs.
4. Twist the logs in braids. Grate the Parmesan cheese.
5. Place the twisted logs in the Ninja Foodi's insert.
6. Sprinkle the grated Parmesan cheese and olive oil, and close the Ninja Foodi's lid.
7. Cook the breadsticks at the "Pressure" mode for 10 minutes.
8. Release the pressure and remove the lid.
9. Leave the breadsticks for 10 minutes to rest.
10. Serve the breadsticks immediately or keep them in a sealed container.

Nutrition:

- InfoCalories: 242; Fat: 18.9g; Carbohydrates: 2.7g; Protein: 11.7g

Cheesy Tomato Bruschetta

Servings: 2
Cooking Time: 15 Min
Ingredients:

- 1 Italian Ciabatta Sandwich Bread
- 2 tomatoes; chopped
- 2 garlic cloves, minced
- 1 cup grated mozzarella cheese /130g
- Olive oil to brush
- Basil leaves; chopped
- Salt and pepper to taste

Directions:

1. Cut the bread in half, lengthways, then each piece again in half. Drizzle each bit with olive oil and sprinkle with garlic. Top with the grated cheese, salt, and pepper.
2. Place the bruschetta pieces into the Ninja Foodi basket, close the crisping lid and cook for 12 minutes on Air Crisp mode at 380 °F or 194°C. At 6 minutes, check for doneness.
3. Once the Ninja Foodi beeps, remove the bruschetta to a serving platter, spoon over the tomatoes and chopped basil to serve.

Chicken Lettuce Wraps

Servings: 6
Cooking Time: 30 Minutes
Ingredients:

- 8 ounces chicken fillet
- ¼ cup tomato juice
- 5 tablespoon sour cream
- 1 teaspoon black pepper
- 8 ounces lettuce leaves
- 1 teaspoon salt
- ½ cup chicken stock
- 1 teaspoon butter
- 1 teaspoon turmeric

Directions:

1. Chop the chicken fillet roughly and sprinkle it with sour cream, tomato juice, black pepper, turmeric, and salt.
2. Mix up the meat mixture. Put the chicken spice mixture in the Ninja Foodi's insert and add chicken stock.
3. Close the Ninja Foodi's lid and cook the dish in the "Sauté" mode for 30 minutes.
4. Once the chicken is done, remove it from the Ninja Foodi's insert and shred it well.
5. Add the butter and blend well. Transfer the shredded chicken to the lettuce leaves.
6. Serve the dish warm.

Nutrition:

- InfoCalories: 138; Fat: 7.4g; Carbohydrates: 12.63g; Protein: 6g

Zucchini Muffins

Servings: 6
Cooking Time: 15 Minutes
Ingredients:

- 1 cup coconut flour
- 1 medium zucchini, finely chopped
- 1 teaspoon baking soda
- 1 tablespoon lemon juice
- ½ teaspoon salt
- ½ teaspoon black pepper
- 1 tablespoon butter
- ⅓ cup of coconut milk
- 1 teaspoon poppy seeds
- 2 tablespoons flax meal

Directions:

1. Place the chopped zucchini in a blender and mix until smooth.
2. Combine the salt, baking soda, lemon juice, poppy, coconut flour, butter, black pepper, and flax meal together.
3. Add the milk and blended zucchini.
4. Knead the dough until smooth. It can be a little bit sticky.
5. Place the muffins in the muffin's tins and transfer the zucchini muffins in the Ninja Foodi's insert.
6. Cook the muffins on the" Steam" mode for 15 minutes.
7. Once done, check if the dish is done using a toothpick.
8. If the muffins are cooked, remove them from the Ninja Foodi's insert and serve.

Nutrition:

- InfoCalories: 146; Fat: 8.9g; Carbohydrates: 13.5g; Protein: 4g

Herbed Cauliflower Fritters

Servings: 7
Cooking Time: 13 Minutes
Ingredients:

- 1-pound cauliflower
- 1 medium white onion
- 1 teaspoon salt
- ½ teaspoon ground white pepper
- 1 tablespoon sour cream
- 1 teaspoon turmeric
- ½ cup dill, chopped
- 1 teaspoon thyme
- 3 tablespoons almond flour
- 1 egg
- 2 tablespoons butter

Directions:

1. Wash the cauliflower and separate it into the florets.
2. Chop the florets and place them in a blender.
3. Peel the onion and dice it. Add the diced onion to a blender and blend the mixture.
4. When you get the smooth texture, add salt, ground white pepper, sour cream, turmeric, dill, thyme, and almond flour.
5. Add egg blend the mixture well until a smooth dough form.
6. Remove the cauliflower dough from a blender and form the medium balls.
7. Flatten the balls a little. Set the Ninja Foodi's insert to" Sauté" mode.
8. Add the butter to the Ninja Foodi's insert and melt it.
9. Add the cauliflower fritters in the Ninja Foodi's insert, and sauté them for 6 minutes.
10. Flip them once. Cook the dish in" Sauté" stew mode for 7 minutes.
11. Once done, remove the fritters from the Ninja Foodi's insert.
12. Serve immediately.

Nutrition:

- InfoCalories: 143; Fat: 10.6g; Carbohydrates: 9.9g; Protein: 5.6g

Chicken Meatballs With Dill Dipping Sauce

Servings: 8

Cooking Time: 15 Minutes

Ingredients:

- Nonstick cooking spray
- 1 lb. lean ground chicken
- 1 tsp oregano
- 1 cup whole wheat panko bread crumbs
- 1 egg, beaten
- 1/3 cup milk
- 2 cloves garlic, diced fine
- 1/3 cup red onions, diced fine
- 1/3 cup fresh parsley, chopped fine
- ¾ tsp salt, divided
- ¼ tsp black pepper
- 1 cup plain Greek yogurt, low fat
- 1/3 cup fresh dill, chopped fine
- 1 lemon, zest and juice
- ½ tsp cumin
- 1/8 tsp cayenne pepper

Directions:

1. Lightly spray the fryer basket with cooking spray.

2. In a large bowl, combine chicken, oregano, bread crumbs, egg, milk, garlic, onions, parsley, ½ teaspoon salt, and black pepper until thoroughly combined. Form into 1-inch meatballs.

3. Place meatballs in the basket in a single layer, do not over crowd. Add the tender crisp lid and set to air fry on 400°F. Cook meatballs 10-15 minutes until cooked through, turning over halfway through cooking time.

4. In a small bowl, stir together yogurt, dill, lemon zest and juice, remaining salt, cumin, and cayenne pepper until combined.

5. Serve meatballs with sauce for dipping.

Nutrition:

- InfoCalories 174,Total Fat 7g,Total Carbs 13g,Protein 14g,Sodium 386mg.

Salmon Croquettes

Servings: 6

Cooking Time: 20 Minutes

Ingredients:

- Nonstick cooking spray
- 14 ¾ oz. pink salmon, drained, bones removed & flaked
- 1 egg
- 2 tbsp. yellow mustard
- 2 tsp fresh parsley, chopped
- ½ tsp onion powder
- ¼ tsp pepper
- ¾ cup herb-seasoned stuffing mix
- ½ cup flour

Directions:

1. Lightly spray fryer basket with cooking spray.

2. In a large bowl, combine salmon, egg, mustard, parsley, onion powder, and pepper and mix well. Form into 12 patties.

3. Place the flour in a shallow dish.

4. Dredge both sides of the patties in the flour and place in the basket in a single layer.

5. Add the tender-crisp lid and set to air fry on 375°F. Cook patties 8-10 minutes per side until gold brown. Serve immediately.

Nutrition:

- InfoCalories 245,Total Fat 7g,Total Carbs 24g,Protein 19g,Sodium 670mg.

Butter-flower Medley

Servings: 10
Cooking Time: 15 Minutes
Ingredients:

- 3 cups butternut squash, peel & cut in 1-inch cubes
- 1 head cauliflower, separated into florets
- 2 cloves garlic
- 1 tbsp. skim milk
- ½ tsp onion powder
- ¼ tsp thyme
- 1/8 tsp salt
- 1/8 tsp black pepper
- 1 tbsp. butter
- 1 tbsp. parmesan cheese, reduced fat

Directions:

1. Add the squash, cauliflower, and garlic to the cooking pot. Pour in ½ cup water. Add the lid and select pressure cooking on high. Set the timer for 8 minutes.
2. When timer goes off use natural release to remove the lid. Drain the vegetables and place in a large bowl.
3. Add remaining ingredients, except parmesan, and beat until smooth.
4. Transfer the squash mixture back to the cooking pot and sprinkle top with parmesan cheese. Add the tender-crisp lid and select air fry on 400°F. Cook 5-6 minutes or until top is lightly browned. Serve.

Nutrition:

- InfoCalories 47,Total Fat 1g,Total Carbs 8g,Protein 2g,Sodium 68mg.

Shallots With Mushrooms

Servings: 7
Cooking Time: 30 Minutes
Ingredients:

- 9 ounces shallot
- 8 ounces mushrooms
- ½ cup chicken stock
- 1 tablespoon paprika
- ½ tablespoon salt
- ¼ cup cream
- 1 teaspoon coriander
- ½ cup dill, chopped
- ½ cup parsley
- 1 tablespoon Erythritol

Directions:

1. Slice the shallot and chop the mushrooms.
2. Combine the chicken stock, salt, paprika, cream, coriander, and Erythritol in a mixing bowl.
3. Blend the mixture well. Chop the dill and parsley.
4. Pour the cream mixture in the Ninja Foodi's insert.
5. Set the Ninja Foodi's insert to" Sauté" mode and add sliced shallot and chopped mushrooms.
6. Blend the mixture using a wooden spoon. Close the Ninja Foodi's lid and sauté the mixture for 30 minutes.
7. Chop the parsley and dill. Once the dish is done, transfer it to serving plates.
8. Sprinkle the cooked dish with the chopped parsley and dill.
9. Do not stir again before serving it.

Nutrition:

- InfoCalories: 52; Fat: 1g; Carbohydrates: 10.2g; Protein: 3g

Saucy Chicken Wings

Servings: 6
Cooking Time: 35 Minutes
Ingredients:

- 1-pound chicken wings
- 1 teaspoon black pepper
- 1 teaspoon tomato paste
- 1 tablespoon garlic, minced
- ⅓ teaspoon soy sauce
- 3 tablespoons olive oil
- 1 teaspoon red pepper
- 1 teaspoon cilantro, chopped
- 1 tablespoon tomato sauce

Directions:

1. Combine the black pepper, red pepper, and cilantro together in a mixing bowl and stir the mixture.
2. Place the chicken wings in a separate bowl and sprinkle the meat with the black pepper mixture.
3. Add tomato paste, minced garlic, soy sauce, and tomato sauce.
4. Coat the chicken completely using your hands.
5. Transfer the meat to the Ninja Foodi's insert.
6. Close the Ninja Foodi's lid and cook the dish in the" Sauté" mode for 35 minutes.
7. Once done, remove the dish from the Ninja Foodi's insert.
8. Serve the chicken wings hot.

Nutrition:

- InfoCalories: 165; Fat: 9.5g; Carbohydrates: 2.02g; Protein: 17g

Spiralized Carrot

Servings: 4
Cooking Time: 13 Minutes
Ingredients:

- 1 cup of water
- 4 big carrots
- 1 teaspoon liquid stevia
- 1 tablespoon turmeric
- 1 tablespoon butter
- ½ teaspoon ground ginger

Directions:

1. Wash and peel the carrots. Use a spiralizer to make the curls or spirals.
2. Put the carrot spirals in the Ninja Foodi's insert.
3. Combine the liquid stevia, water, turmeric, and ground ginger together in a mixing bowl.
4. Stir the mixture well. Set the Ninja Foodi's insert to" Sauté" mode.
5. Add the butter to the carrot mixture and sauté it for 3 minutes.
6. Stir the vegetables frequently. Add the stevia mixture and Close the Ninja Foodi's lid.
7. Cook the dish on" Sauté" mode for 10 minutes.
8. Once the carrot spirals are cooked, remove them from the Ninja Foodi's insert, strain them from the stevia liquid.
9. Serve.

Nutrition:

- InfoCalories: 62; Fat: 3.1g; Carbohydrates: 8.3g; Protein: 0.8g

Chapter 7 Desserts

Classic Custard

Servings: 4

Cooking Time: 30 Minutes

Ingredients:

- Nonstick cooking spray
- 4 eggs
- ½ cup half and half
- 2 cups almond milk, unsweetened
- 1/3 cup Stevia
- 1 tsp vanilla
- ¼ tsp cinnamon

Directions:

1. Spray four ramekins with cooking spray.
2. In a large bowl, whisk all the ingredients together until combined. Pour into prepared ramekins
3. Place the ramekins in the cooking pot and pour enough water around them it comes ½ inch up the sides of the ramekins.
4. Add the tender-crisp lid and set to bake on 350°F. Bake 30 minutes or until custard is set. Transfer to a wire rack and let cool before serving.

Nutrition:

- InfoCalories 135,Total Fat 5g,Total Carbs 23g,Protein 11g,Sodium 164mg.

Raspberry Lemon Cheesecake

Servings: 8

Cooking Time: 30 Minutes

Ingredients:

- Butter flavored cooking spray
- 8 oz. cream cheese, fat free, soft
- 1/3 cup sugar
- ½ tsp lemon juice
- 1 tsp lemon zest
- ½ tsp vanilla
- ½ cup plain Greek yogurt
- 2 eggs, room temperature
- 2 tbsp. white whole wheat flour
- Fresh raspberries for garnish

Directions:

1. Spray an 8-inch baking dish with cooking spray.
2. In a large bowl, beat cream cheese, sugar, lemon juice, zest, and vanilla until smooth.
3. Add yogurt, eggs, and flour and mix well. Spoon into prepared pan.
4. Place pan in the cooking pot and add the tender-crisp lid. Set to bake on 350°F. Bake 25-30 minutes or until cheesecake passes the toothpick test.
5. Transfer to a wire rack to cool. Cover with plastic wrap and refrigerate 2-3 hours. Serve garnished with fresh raspberries.

Nutrition:

- InfoCalories 93,Total Fat 6g,Total Carbs 14g,Protein 5g,Sodium 127mg.

Delicious Almond And Apple

Servings: 4

Cooking Time: 14 Min

Ingredients:

- 3 Apples, peeled and diced
- ½ cup Milk /125ml
- ½ cup Almonds; chopped or slivered /65g
- ¼ tsp Cinnamon /1.25g

Directions:

1. Place all ingredients in the Foodi. Stir well to combine and seal the pressure lid. Cook on Pressure for 4 minutes at High. Release the pressure quickly. Divide the mixture among 4 serving bowls.

Fried Oreos

Servings:9

Cooking Time: 8 Minutes

Ingredients:

- ½ cup complete pancake mix
- ⅓ cup water
- Cooking spray
- 9 Oreo cookies
- 1 tablespoon confectioners' sugar

Directions:

1. Close crisping lid. Select AIR CRISP, set temperature to 400°F, and set time to 5 minutes. Select START/STOP to begin preheating.
2. In a medium bowl, combine the pancake mix and water until combined.
3. Spray the Cook & Crisp Basket with cooking spray.
4. Dip each cookie into the pancake batter and then arrange them in the basket in a single layer so they are not touching each other. Cook in batches if needed.
5. When unit has preheated, open lid and insert basket into pot. Close crisping lid.
6. Select AIR CRISP, set temperature to 400°F, and set time to 8 minutes. Select START/STOP to begin.
7. After 4 minutes, open lid and flip the cookies. Close lid and continue cooking.
8. When cooking is complete, check for desired crispness. Remove basket and sprinkle the cookies with confectioners' sugar. Serve.

Nutrition:

- InfoCalories: 83,Total Fat: 2g,Sodium: 158mg,Carbohydrates: 14g,Protein: 1g.

Vanilla Hot Lava Cake

Servings: 8
Cooking Time: 40 Min
Ingredients:

- 1 ½ cups chocolate chips /195g
- 1 ½ cups sugar /195g
- 1 cup butter /130g
- 1 cup water /250ml
- 5 eggs
- 7 tbsp flour/105g
- 4 tbsp milk /60ml
- 4 tsp vanilla extract /20ml
- Powdered sugar to garnish

Directions:

1. Grease the cake pan with cooking spray and set aside. Open the Foodi, fit the reversible rack at the bottom of it, and pour in the water. In a medium heatproof bowl, add the butter and chocolate and melt them in the microwave for about 2 minutes. Remove it from the microwave.

2. Add sugar and use a spatula to stir it well. Add the eggs, milk, and vanilla extract and stir again. Finally, add the flour and stir it until even and smooth.

3. Pour the batter into the greased cake pan and use the spatula to level it. Place the pan on the trivet in the pot, close the lid, secure the pressure valve, and select Pressure on High for 15 minutes. Press Start/Stop.

4. Once the timer has gone off, do a natural pressure release for 10 minutes, then a quick pressure release, and open the lid.

5. Remove the rack with the pan on it and place the pan on a flat surface. Put a plate over the pan and flip the cake over into the plate. Pour the powdered sugar in a fine sieve and sift it over the cake. Use a knife to cut the cake into 8 slices and serve immediately (while warm).

Apple Strudels

Servings: 8
Cooking Time: 25 Minutes
Ingredients:

- Butter flavored cooking spray
- 2 8 oz. whole grain puff pastry sheets
- 5 apples, cored, peeled & chopped
- ¼ cup raisins
- 1/8 cup pine nuts
- 1 tbsp. Stevia
- 1 tbsp. lemon zest
- ½ tsp cinnamon
- 1 egg

Directions:

1. Lightly spray the fryer basket with cooking spray.

2. Lay the puff pastry on a work surface and cut into 4 equal parts. Repeat with the second sheet.

3. In a large bowl, combine apples, raisins, pine nuts, Stevia, zest, and cinnamon and mix well. Spoon filling into center of each pastry piece. Fold over sides and roll up.

4. In a small bowl, whisk the egg. Place the pastries in the fryer basket in a single layer. Brush tops with egg.

5. Add the tender-crisp lid and set to air fry on 350°F. Bake 20-25 minutes or until puffed and golden brown. Serve immediately.

Nutrition:

- InfoCalories 376,Total Fat 23g,Total Carbs 17g,Protein 5g,Sodium 141mg.

Pineapple Cake

Servings: 4

Cooking Time: 50 Min

Ingredients:

- 2 oz. dark chocolate, grated /60g
- 4 oz. butter /120g
- 7 oz. pineapple chunks /210g
- 8 oz. self-rising flour /240g
- ½ cup sugar /65g
- 1 egg
- ½ cup pineapple juice /125ml
- 2 tbsp milk /30ml

Directions:

1. Preheat the Foodi to 390 °F or 199°C. Place the butter and flour into a bowl and rub the mixture with your fingers until crumbed. Stir in the pineapple, sugar, chocolate, and juice. Beat the eggs and milk separately, and then add them to the batter.

2. Transfer the batter to a previously prepared (greased or lined) cake pan, and cook for 40 minutes on Roast mode. Let cool for at least 10 minutes before serving.

Maply Soufflés

Servings: 4

Cooking Time: 10 Minutes

Ingredients:

- Butter flavored cooking spray
- 1/3 cup maple syrup
- 2 eggs, separated
- ½ tsp vanilla
- 2 tbsp. flour
- 1/8 tsp salt
- Powdered sugar for dusting

Directions:

1. Spray 4 ramekins with cooking spray.

2. In a medium bowl, beat syrup, egg yolks, and vanilla until thickened, about 1 minute.

3. Add flour and beat until combined.

4. In a large bowl, beat egg whites until stiff peaks form, about 2 minutes. Gently fold ¼ of the egg whites into syrup mixture just until combined. Fold the syrup mixture into the remaining egg whites just until combined. Divide evenly among ramekins.

5. Place ramekins in the cooking pot and add the tender-crisp lid. Set to bake on 375°F. Bake 10-12 minutes, or until puffed and golden brown. Dust with powdered sugar and serve immediately.

Nutrition:

- InfoCalories 119,Total Fat 2g,Total Carbs 21g,Protein 3g,Sodium 116mg.

Pumpkin Crème Brulee

Servings: 4
Cooking Time: 3:00 Hours
Ingredients:

- 1 egg yolk
- 1 egg, lightly beaten
- ¾ cup heavy cream
- 4 tbsp. pumpkin puree
- 1 tsp vanilla
- 4 tbsp. sugar, divided
- ¾ tsp pumpkin pie spice

Directions:

1. In a medium bowl, whisk together egg yolk and beaten egg, mix well.
2. Whisk in cream, slowly until combined.
3. Stir in pumpkin and vanilla and mix until combined.
4. In a small bowl, stir together 2 tablespoons sugar and pie spice. Add to pumpkin mixture and stir to blend.
5. Fill 4 small ramekins with mixture and place in the cooking pot. Carefully pour water around the ramekins, it should reach halfway up the sides.
6. Add the lid and set to slow cooking on low. Cook 2-3 hours or until custard is set.
7. Sprinkle remaining 2 tablespoons over the top of the custards. Add the tender-crisp lid and set to broil on 450°F. Cook another 2-3 minutes or until sugar caramelizes, be careful not to let it burn. Transfer ramekins to wire rack to cool before serving.

Nutrition:

- InfoCalories 334,Total Fat 21g,Total Carbs 30g,Protein 6g,Sodium 59mg.

Blueberry Peach Crisp

Servings: 8
Cooking Time: 40 Minutes
Ingredients:

- 1 cup blueberries
- 6 peaches, peeled, cored & cut in ½-inch pieces
- ½ cup + 3 tbsp. flour
- ¾ cups Stevia, divided
- ½ tsp cinnamon
- ¼ tsp salt, divided
- Zest & juice of 1 lemon
- 1 cup oats
- 1/3 cup coconut oil, melted

Directions:

1. Place the rack in the cooking pot.
2. In a large bowl, combine blueberries, peaches, 3 tablespoons flour, ¼ cup Stevia, cinnamon, and 1/8 teaspoon salt, toss to coat fruit. Stir in lemon zest and juice just until combined. Pour into an 8-inch baking dish.
3. In a medium bowl, combine oats, ½ cup Stevia, coconut oil, remaining flour and salt and mix with a fork until crumbly. Sprinkle over the top of the fruit.
4. Place the dish on the rack and add the tender-crisp lid. Set to bake on 350 °F. Bake 35-40 minutes until filling is bubbly and top is golden brown. Serve warm.

Nutrition:

- InfoCalories 265,Total Fat 11g,Total Carbs 44g,Protein 6g,Sodium 74mg.

Coconut Milk Crème Caramel

Servings: 4

Cooking Time: 20 Min

Ingredients:

- 7 ounces Condensed Coconut Milk /210ml
- 1 ½ cups Water /375ml
- ½ cup Coconut Milk /125ml
- 2 Eggs
- ½ tsp Vanilla /2.5ml
- 4 tbsp Caramel Syrup /60ml

Directions:

1.   Divide the caramel syrup between 4 small ramekins. Pour water in the Foodi and add the reversible rack. In a bowl, beat the rest of the ingredients. Divide them between the ramekins. Cover them with aluminum foil and lower onto the reversible rack.

2.   Seal the pressure lid, and choose Pressure, set to High, and set the time to 15 minutes. Press Start. Once cooking is completed, do a quick pressure release. Let cool completely. To unmold the flan, insert a spatula along the ramekin' sides and flip onto a dish.

Molten Lava Cake

Servings: 4

Cooking Time: 20 Min

Ingredients:

- 3 ½ oz. butter, melted /105ml
- 3 ½ oz. dark chocolate, melted /105ml
- 2 eggs
- 3 ½ tbsp sugar /52.5g
- 1 ½ tbsp self-rising flour /22.5g

Directions:

1.   Grease 4 ramekins with butter. Beat the eggs and sugar until frothy. Stir in the butter and chocolate.

2.   Gently fold in the flour. Divide the mixture between the ramekins and bake in the Foodi for 10 minutes on Air Crisp mode at 370 °F or 188°C. Let cool for 2 minutes before turning the lava cakes upside down onto serving plates.

Chocolaty Fudge

Servings: 8

Cooking Time: 55 Min

Ingredients:

- 1 oz. cocoa powder /30g
- 4 oz. butter /120g
- 7 oz. flour, sifted /210g
- 1 cup sugar /130g
- ¼ cup milk /62.5ml
- 2 eggs
- 1 tbsp honey /15ml
- 1 tsp vanilla extract /5ml
- 1 orange, juice and zest
- Icing:
- 4 oz. powdered sugar /120g
- 1 oz. butter, melted /30ml
- 1 tbsp milk /15ml
- 1 tbsp brown sugar/15g
- 2 tsp honey /10ml

Directions:

1. In a bowl, mix the dry ingredients for the fudge. Mix the wet ingredients separately. Combine the two mixtures gently. Transfer the batter to a prepared Foodi basket. Close the crisping lid and cook for about 35 minutes on Roast mode at 350 °F or 177°C.

2. Once the timer beeps, check to ensure the cake is cooked. For the Topping: whisk together all of the icing ingredients. When the cake is cooled, coat it with the icing. Let set before slicing the fudge.

Chocolate Fondue

Servings: 12

Cooking Time: 5 Min

Ingredients:

- 10 ounces Milk Chocolate; chopped into small pieces /300g
- 1 ½ cups Lukewarm Water /375ml
- 8 ounces Heavy Whipping Cream /240ml
- 2 tsp Coconut Liqueur /60ml
- ¼ tsp Cinnamon Powder /1.25g
- A pinch of Salt

Directions:

1. Melt the chocolate in a heat-proof recipient. Add the remaining ingredients, except for the liqueur. Transfer this recipient to the metal reversible rack. Pour 1 ½ cups or 375ml of water into the cooker, and place a reversible rack inside.

2. Seal the pressure lid, choose Pressure, set to High, and set the time to 5 minutes. Press Start. Once the cooking is complete, do a quick pressure release. Pull out the container with tongs. Mix in the coconut liqueur and serve right now. Enjoy!

Chocolate Blackberry Cake

Servings: 10
Cooking Time: 3 Hours
Ingredients:

- 2 cups almond flour
- 1 cup unsweetened coconut, shredded
- ½ cup Erythritol
- ¼ cup unsweetened Protein: powder
- 2 teaspoons baking soda
- ¼ teaspoon salt
- 4 large eggs
- ½ cup heavy cream
- ½ cup unsalted butter, melted
- 1 cup fresh blackberries
- 1/3 cup 70% dark chocolate chips

Directions:

1. Grease the Ninja Foodi's insert.
2. In a suitable, mix together the flour, coconut, Erythritol Protein: powder, baking soda and salt.
3. In another large bowl, stir in the eggs, cream and butter and beat until well combined.
4. Stir in the dry flour mixture and mix until well combined.
5. Fold in the blackberries and chocolate chips.
6. In the prepared Ninja Foodi's insert, add the mixture.
7. Close the Ninja Foodi's lid with a crisping lid and select "Slow Cooker".
8. Set on "Low" for 3 hours.
9. Press the "Start/Stop" button to initiate cooking.
10. Transfer the pan onto a wire rack about 10 minutes.
11. Flip the baked and cooled cake onto the wire rack to cool completely.
12. Cut into desired-sized slices and serve.

Nutrition:

- InfoCalories: 305; Fats: 27.5g; Carbohydrates: 7.7g; Proteins: 10.6g

Moon Milk

Servings: 2
Cooking Time: 10 Min
Ingredients:

- 1/4 cup hemp hearts /32.5g
- 1 cup milk /250ml
- 1 pinch ground nutmeg
- 1 pinch ground ginger
- 1 pinch freshly ground black pepper
- ½ tsp maca powder /2.5g
- 1/8 tsp ground cardamom/0.625g
- ½ tsp ground cinnamon, plus more for garnish /2.5g
- 1 tsp coconut oil /5ml
- ½ tsp ground turmeric /2.5g
- 1 tsp honey /5ml

Directions:

1. To the Foodi, add milk. Press Sear/Sauté and heat the milk for 3-4 minutes until the point of starting to bubble; stir in coconut oil, turmeric, nutmeg, pepper, ginger, hemp hearts, maca powder, cinnamon, and cardamom.
2. Press Start/Stop and allow mixture to cool for about a minute; whisk in honey. Transfer the mixture into a mug. Add more cinnamon for garnishing!

Carrot Raisin Cookie Bars

Servings: 16

Cooking Time: 15 Minutes

Ingredients:

- Butter flavored cooking spray
- ½ cup brown sugar
- ½ cup sugar
- ½ cup coconut oil, melted
- ½ cup applesauce, unsweetened
- 2 eggs
- 1 tsp vanilla
- ½ cup almond flour
- 1 tsp baking soda
- 1 tsp baking powder
- ¼ tsp salt
- 1 tsp cinnamon
- ½ tsp nutmeg
- ½ tsp ginger
- 2 cups oats
- 1 ½ cups carrots, finely grated
- 1 cup raisins

Directions:

1. Place the rack in the cooking pot. Spray an 8x8-inch pan with cooking spray.
2. In a large bowl, combine sugars, oil, applesauce, eggs, and vanilla, mix well.
3. Stir in dry ingredients until combined. Fold in carrots and raisins. Press evenly in prepared pan.
4. Place the pan on the rack and add the tender-crisp lid. Set to bake on 350°F. Bake 12-15 minutes or until golden brown and cooked through.
5. Remove to wire rack to cool before cutting and serving.

Nutrition:

- InfoCalories 115,Total Fat 7g,Total Carbs 19g,Protein 3g,Sodium 56mg.

Yogurt Cheesecake

Servings: 8
Cooking Time: 40 Minutes
Ingredients:

- 4 cups plain Greek Yogurt
- 1 cup Erythritol
- ½ teaspoon vanilla extract

Directions:

1. Line a cake pans with Parchment paper.
2. In a suitable, stir in the yogurt and Erythritol and with a hand mixer, mix well.
3. Stir in vanilla extract and mix to combine.
4. Add the mixture into the prepared pan and cover with a paper kitchen towel.
5. Then with a piece of foil, cover the pan tightly.
6. In the Ninja Foodi's insert, place 1 cup of water.
7. Set a "Reversible Rack" in the Ninja Foodi's insert.
8. Place the ramekins over the "Reversible Rack".
9. Close the Ninja Foodi's lid with a pressure lid and place the pressure valve to the "Seal" position.
10. Select "Pressure" mode and set it to "High" for 40 minutes.
11. Press the "Start/Stop" button to initiate cooking.
12. Switch the pressure valve to "Vent" and do a "Quick" release.
13. Place the pan onto a wire rack and remove the foil and paper towel.
14. Again, cover the pan with a new paper towel and refrigerate to cool overnight.

Nutrition:

- InfoCalories: 88; Fats: 1.5g; Carbohydrates: 8.7g; Proteins: 7g

Gingery Chocolate Pudding

Servings: 4
Cooking Time: 20 Min
Ingredients:

- 2 oz. chocolate, coarsely chopped /60g
- 1 ½ cups of Water /375ml
- ¼ cup Cornstarch /32.5g
- 1 cup Almond Milk /250ml
- ¼ cup Sugar /32.5g
- 3 Eggs, separated into whites and yolks
- Zest and Juice from ½ Lime
- 2 tbsp Butter, softened /30g
- ½ tsp Ginger, caramelized /2.5g
- A pinch of Salt

Directions:

1. Combine together the sugar, cornstarch, salt, and softened butter, in a bowl. Mix in lime juice and grated lime zest. Add in the egg yolks, ginger, almond milk, and whisk to mix well.
2. Mix in egg whites. Pour this mixture into custard cups and cover with aluminium foil. Add 1 ½ cups or 375ml of water to the Foodi. Place a reversible rack into the Foodi, and lower the cups onto the rack.
3. Seal the pressure lid, choose Pressure, set to High, and set the time to 25 minutes. Press Start. Once the cooking is complete, do a quick pressure release. Carefully open the pressure lid, and stir in the chocolate. Serve chilled.

Blueberry Muffins

Servings: 10

Cooking Time: 30 Min

Ingredients:

- 1 cup blueberries /130g
- 1 ½ cup flour /195g
- ½ cup sugar /65g
- ¼ cup vegetable oil /62.5ml
- 1 egg
- 2 tsp vanilla extract /10ml
- 2 tsp baking powder /10g
- ½ tsp salt /2.5g
- Yogurt, as needed

Directions:

1. Combine all the flour, salt and baking powder in a bowl. In a bowl, place the oil, vanilla extract, and egg. Fill the rest of the bowl with yogurt.

2. Whisk the mixture until fully incorporated. Combine the wet and dry ingredients. Gently fold in the blueberries. Divide the mixture between 10 muffin cups.

3. You may need to cook in batches. Close the crisping lid and cook for 10 minutes on Air Crisp mode at 350 °F or 177°C, until nice and crispy.

INDEX

Mississippi Pot Roast With Potatoes 57

Molten Lava Cake 108

Moon Milk 110

Mushroom Goulash 29

Mushroom Leek Soup With Parmesan Croutons 24

Mussel Chowder With Oyster Crackers 77

O

Orecchiette And Pork Ragu 66

P

Parmesan Breadsticks 97

Parmesan Stuffed Mushrooms 93

Parmesan Tilapia 69

Peanut Butter Banana Baked Oatmeal 18

Peanut Tofu & Noodles 30

Pepperoni Omelets 15

Pineapple Cake 106

Pistachio Crusted Salmon 73

Polynesian Pork Burger 62

Pork Chops With Squash Purée And Mushroom Gravy 63

Potato Chowder With Peppery Prawns 76

Pumpkin Coconut Breakfast Bake 16

Pumpkin Crème Brulee 107

Pumpkin Soup 21

Q

Quick Indian-style Curry 26

R

Raspberry Lemon Cheesecake 103

Rosemary Lemon Chicken 47

Rosemary Potato Fries 90

S

Salmon Chowder 73

Salmon Croquettes 100

Salmon Kale Meal 85

Saucy Chicken Wings 102

Sausage & Broccoli Frittata 12

Sesame Tuna Steaks 79

Shallots With Mushrooms 101

Short Ribs With Egg Noodles 65

Shredded Chicken & Black Beans 46

Shrimp & Asparagus Risotto 83

Shrimp & Zoodles 80

Printed in Great Britain
by Amazon

11714871R00068